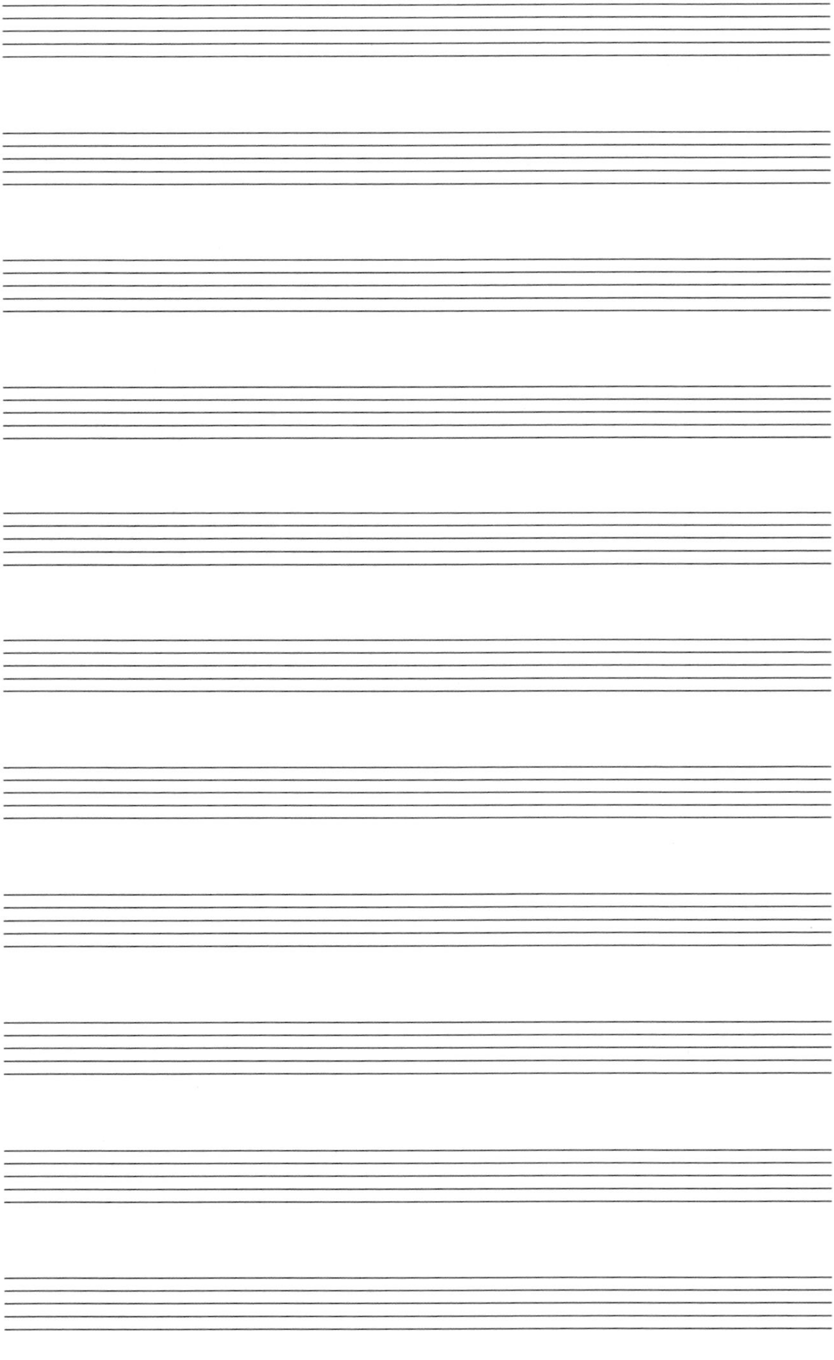

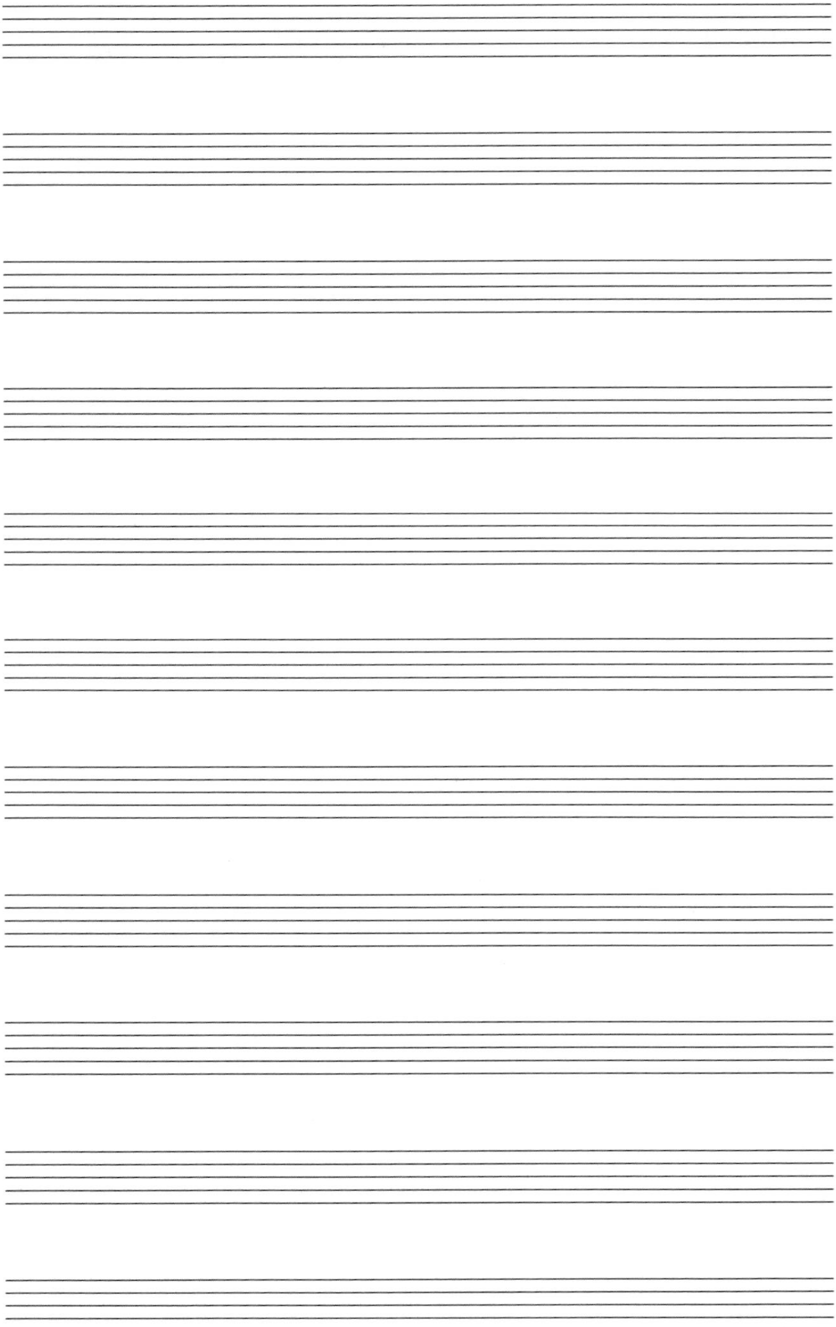

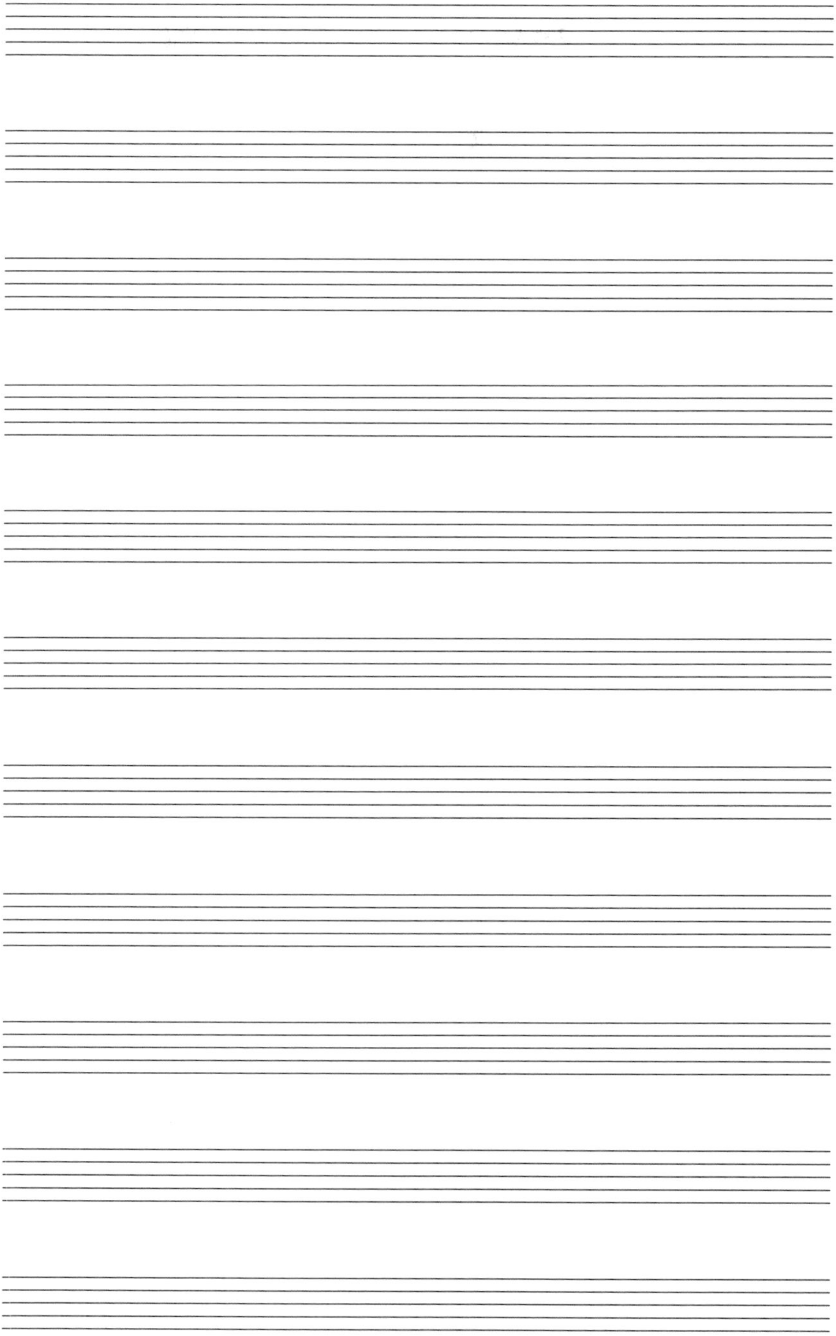

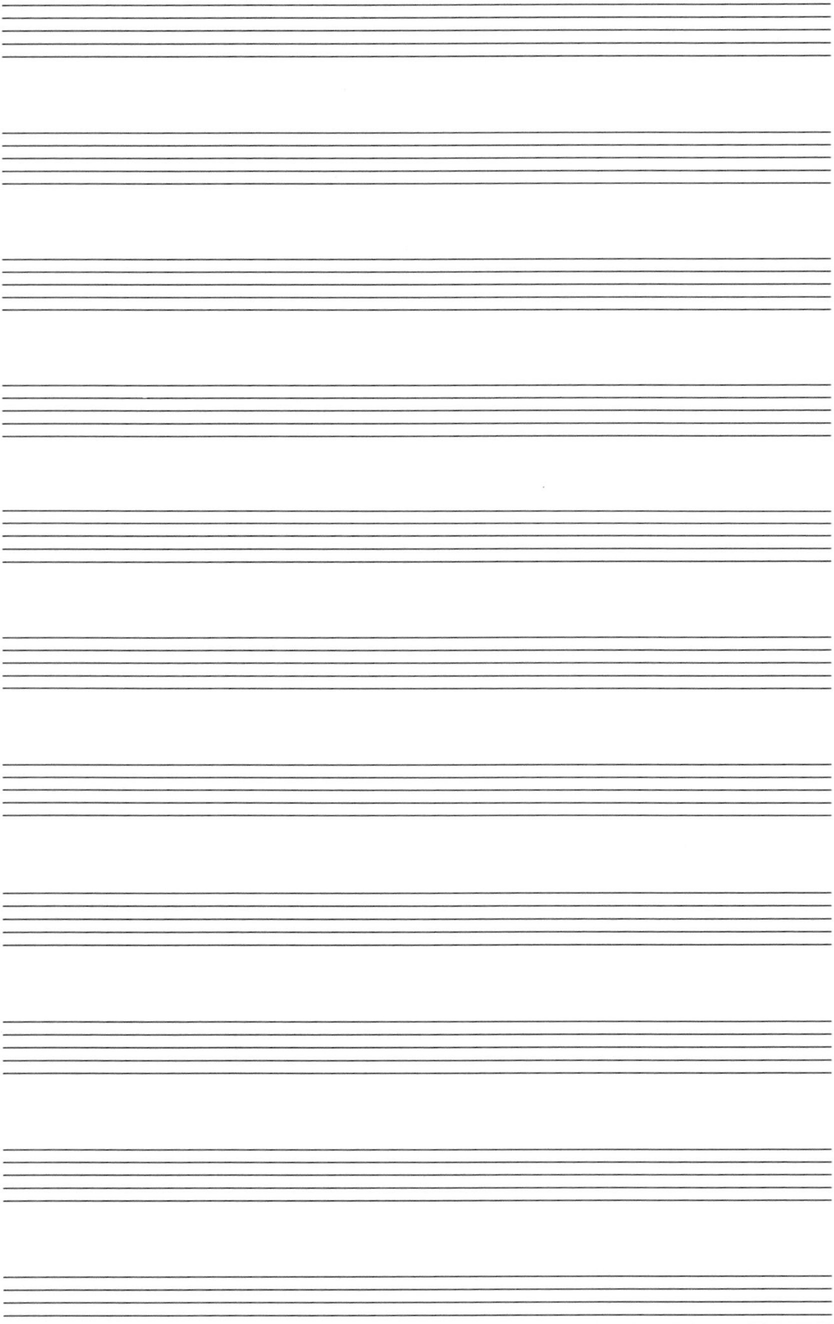

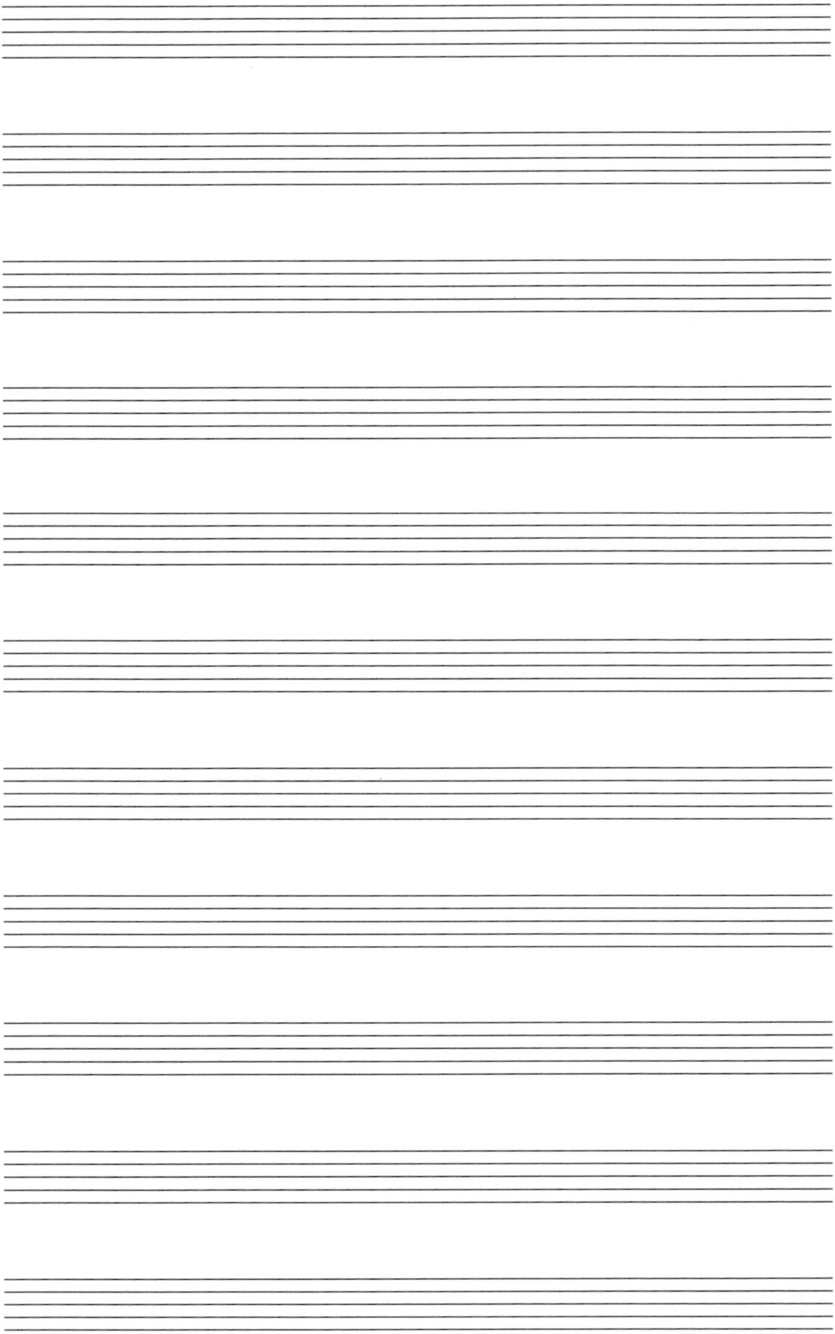

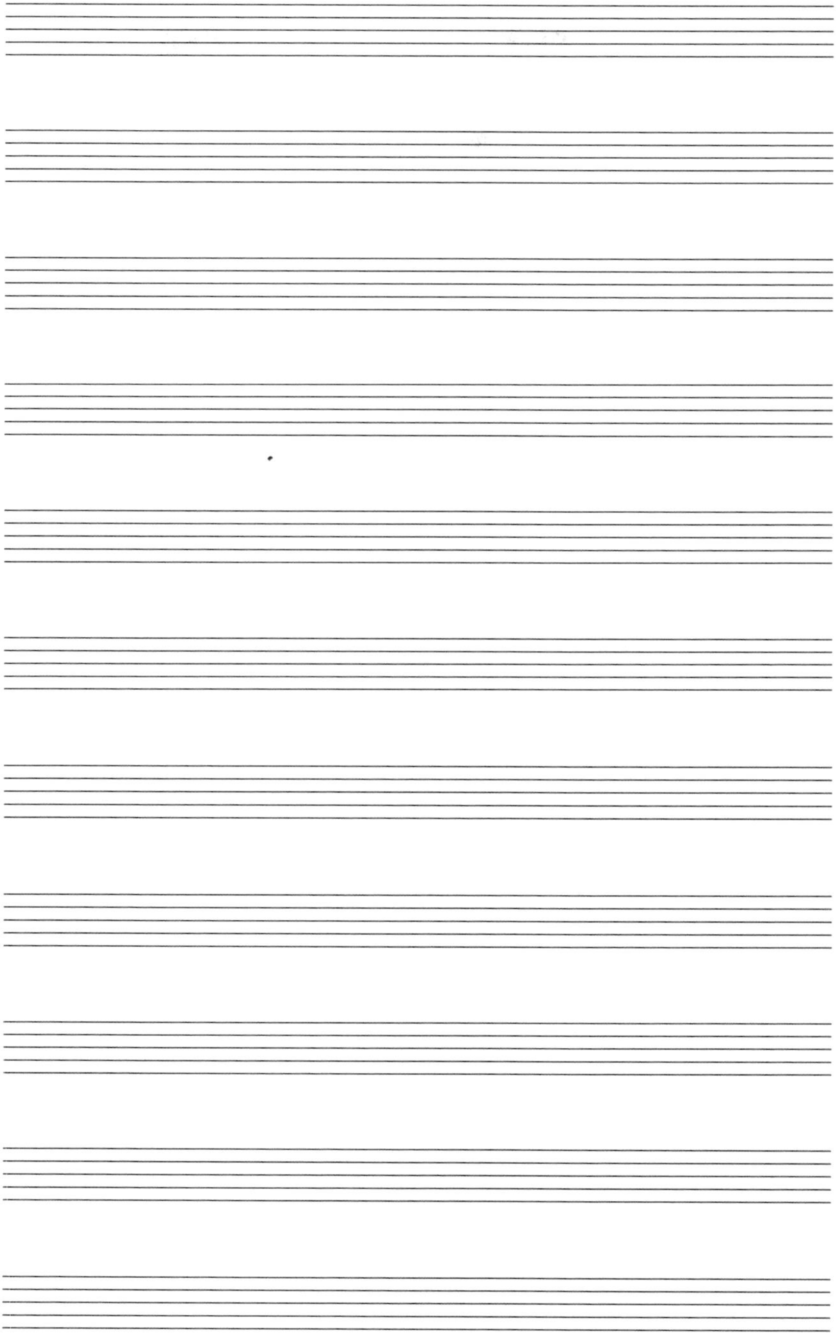

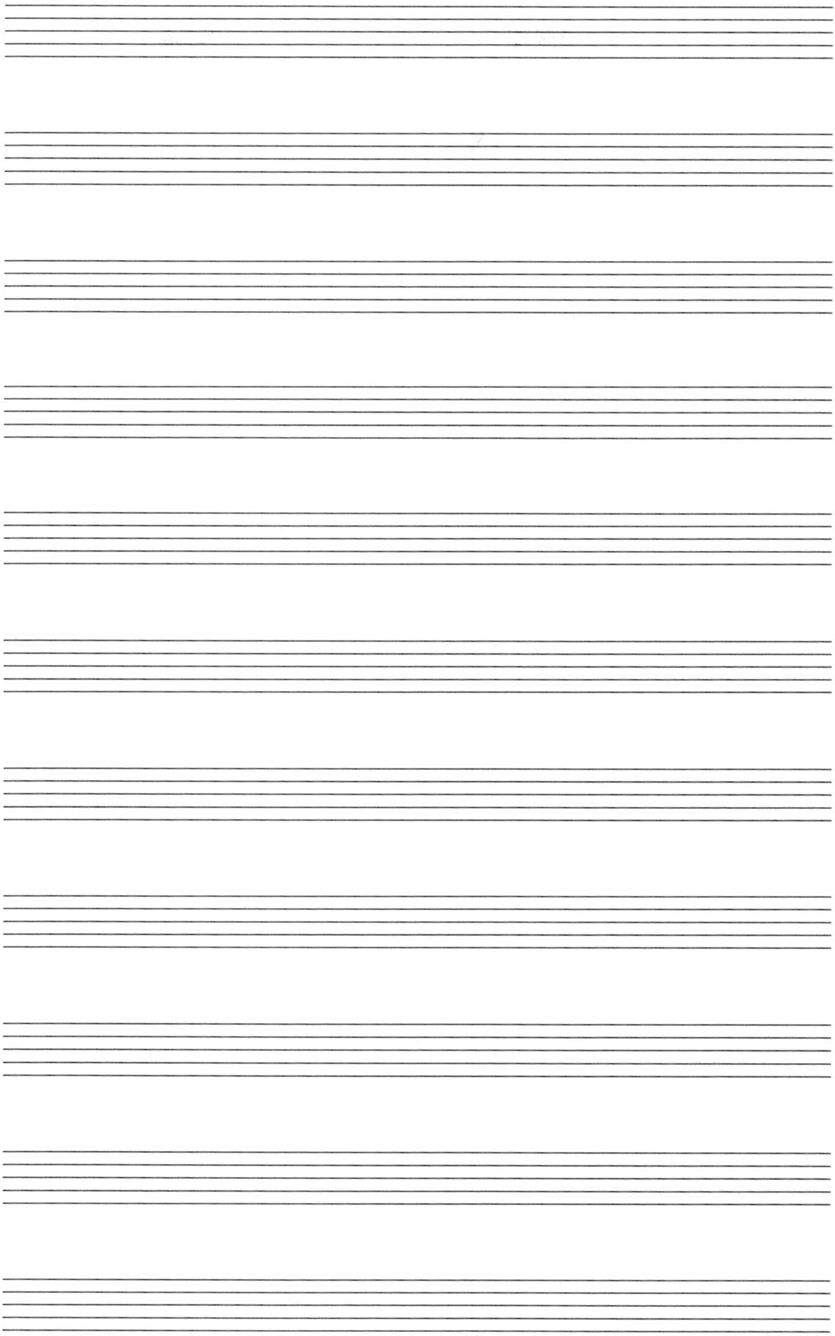

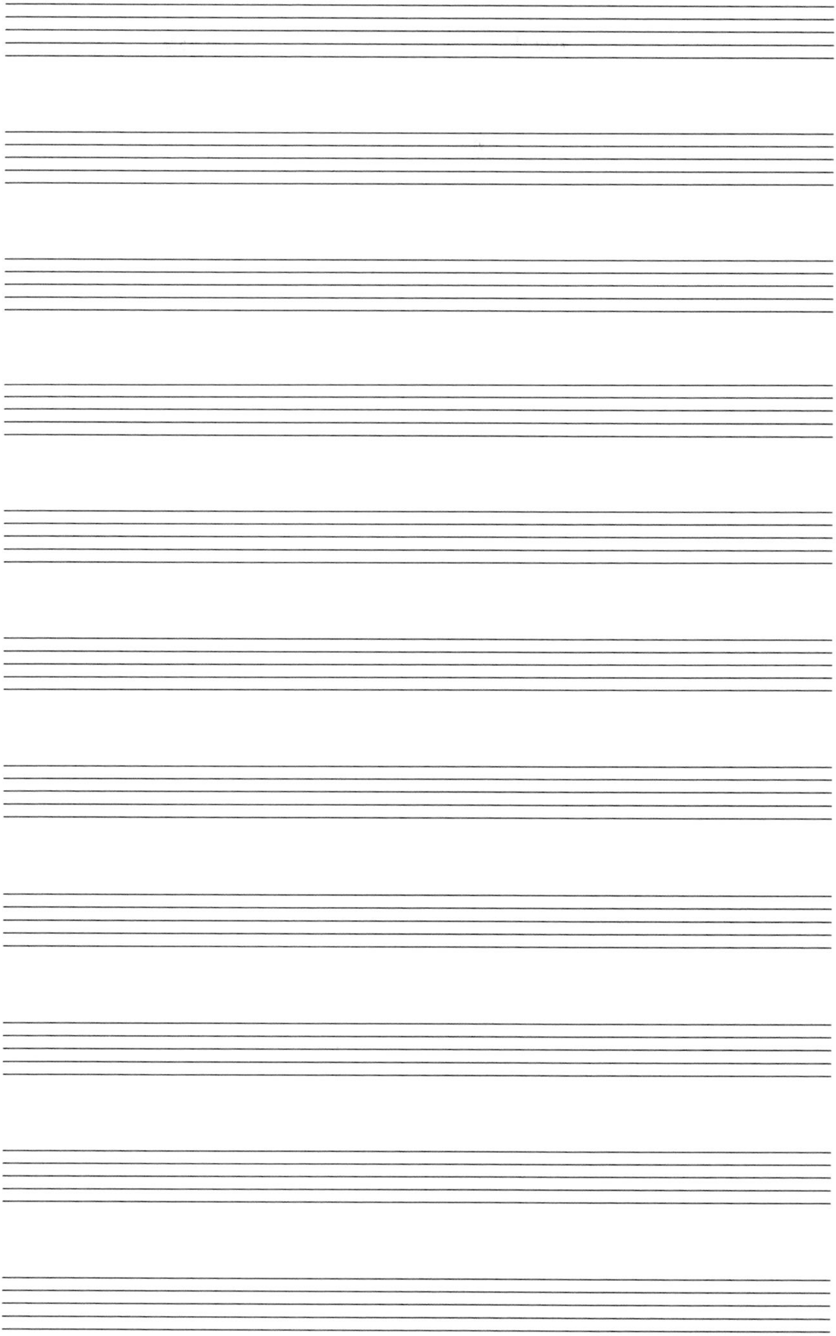

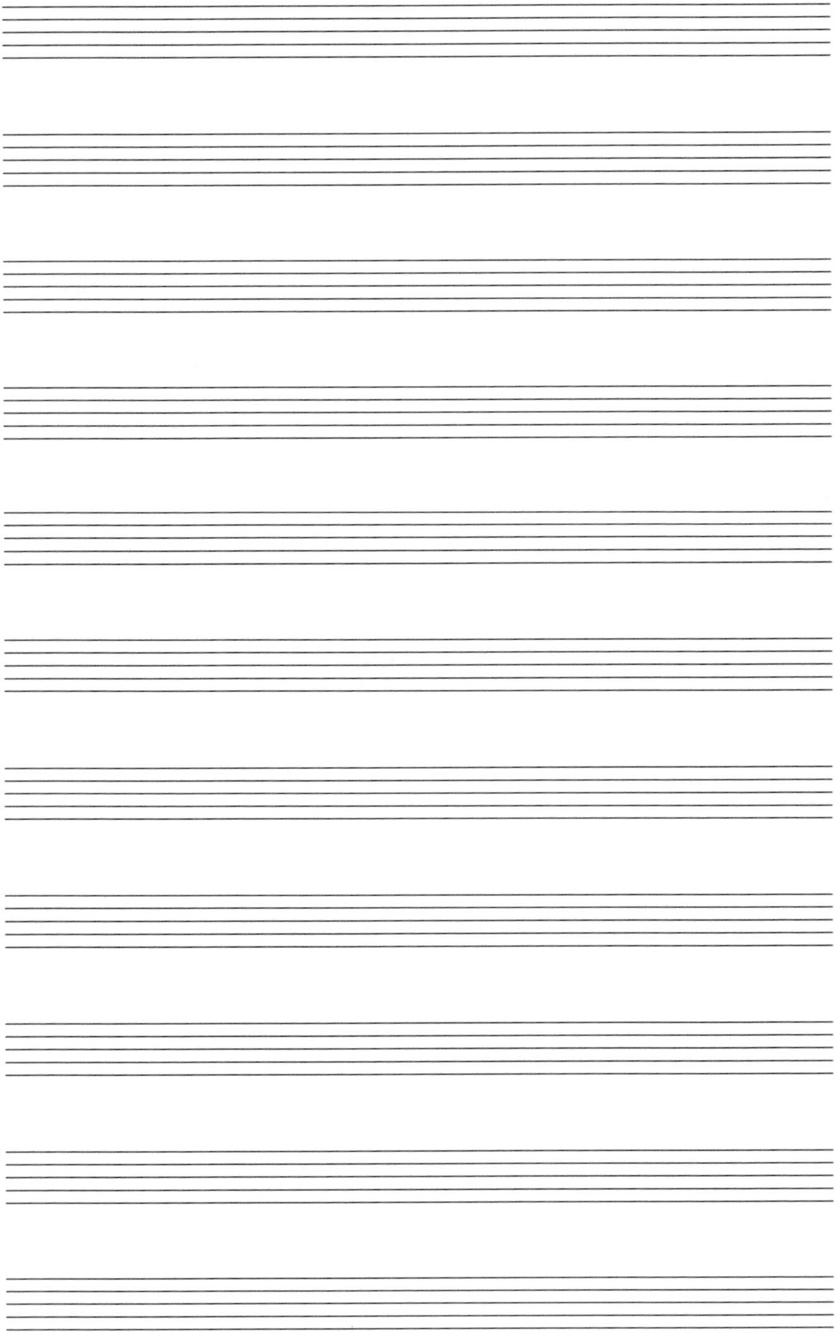

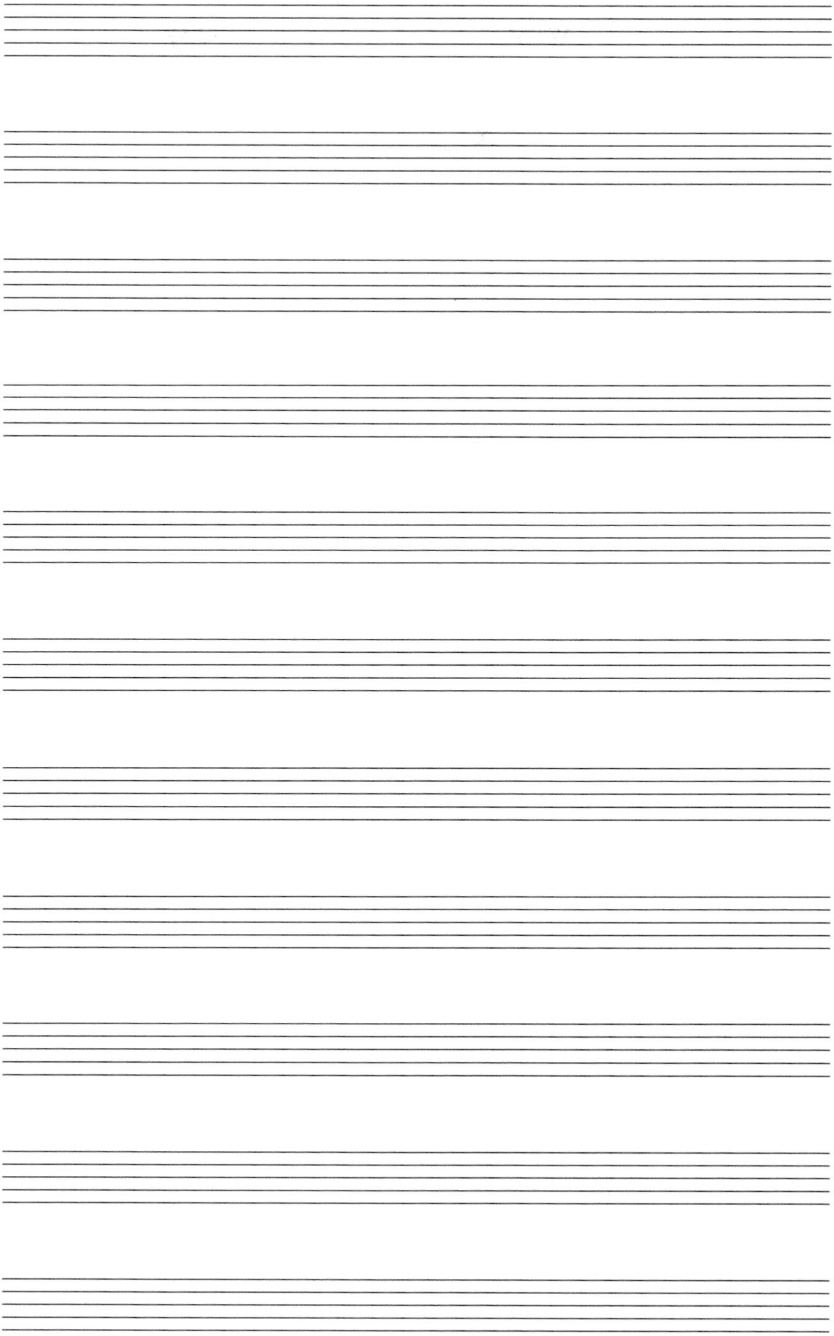

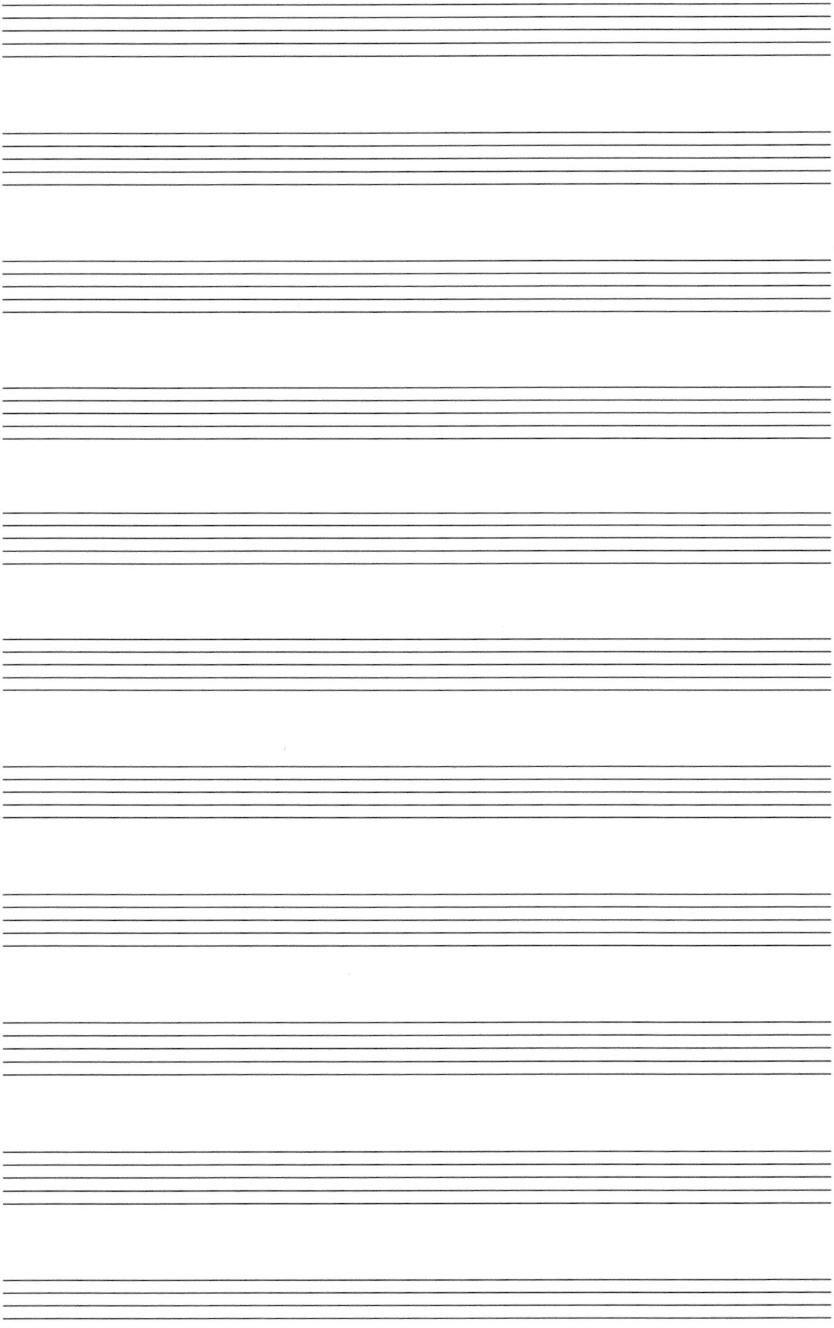

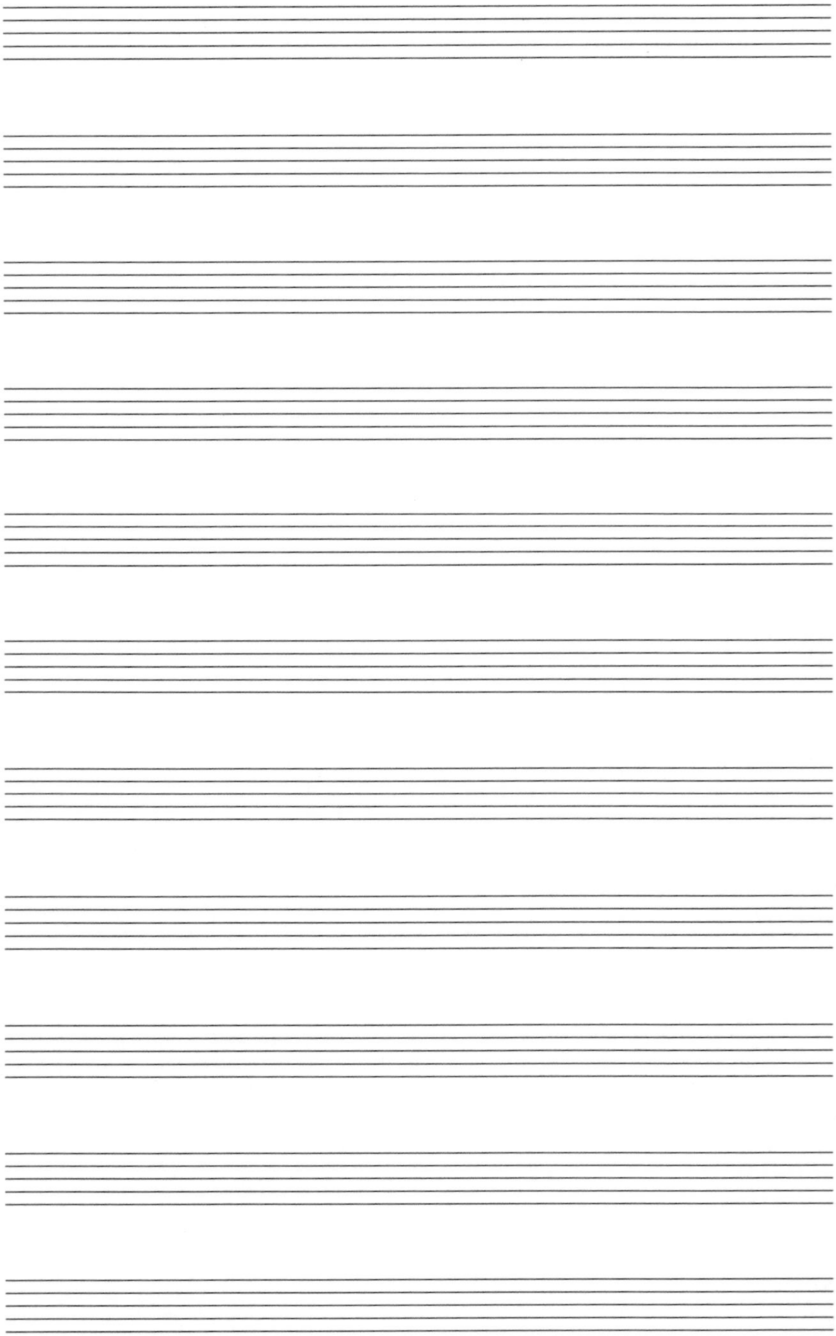

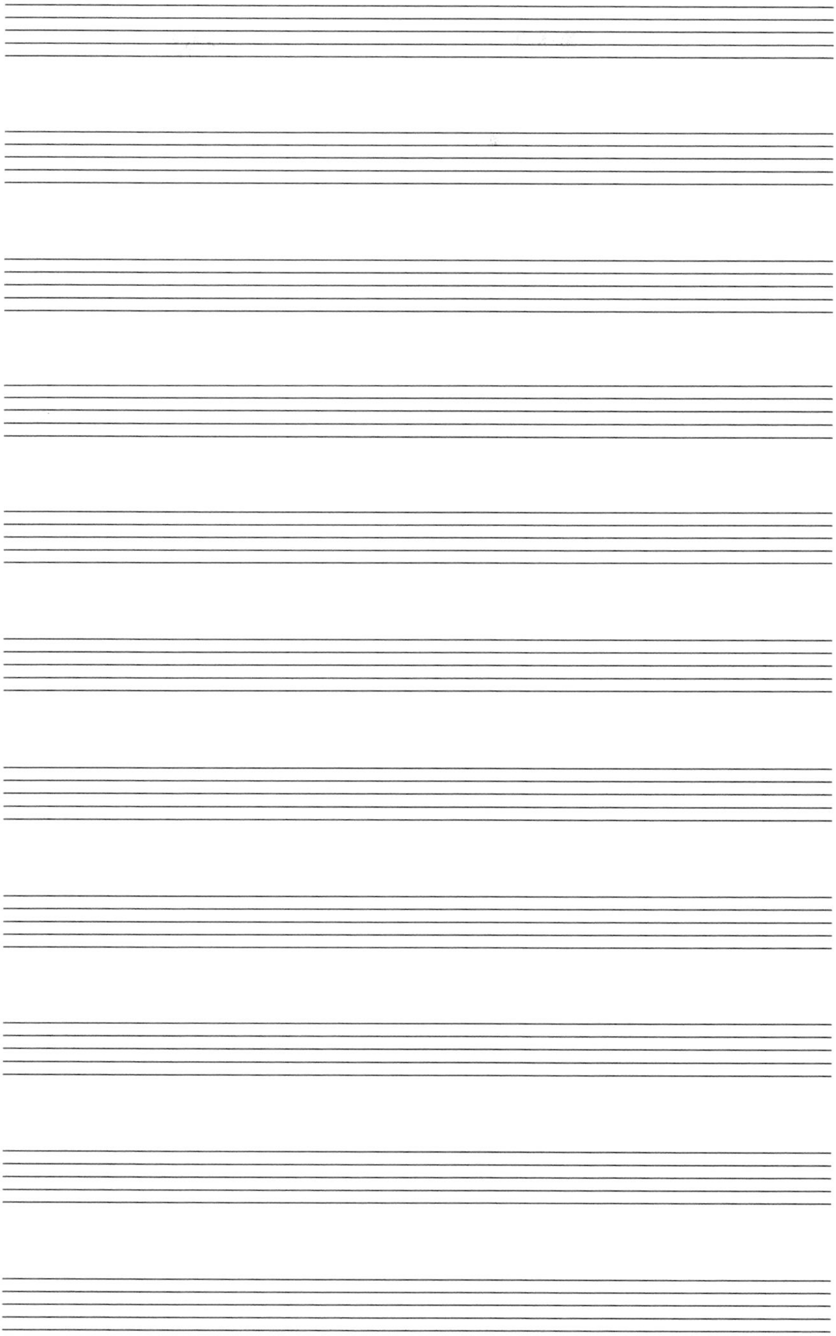

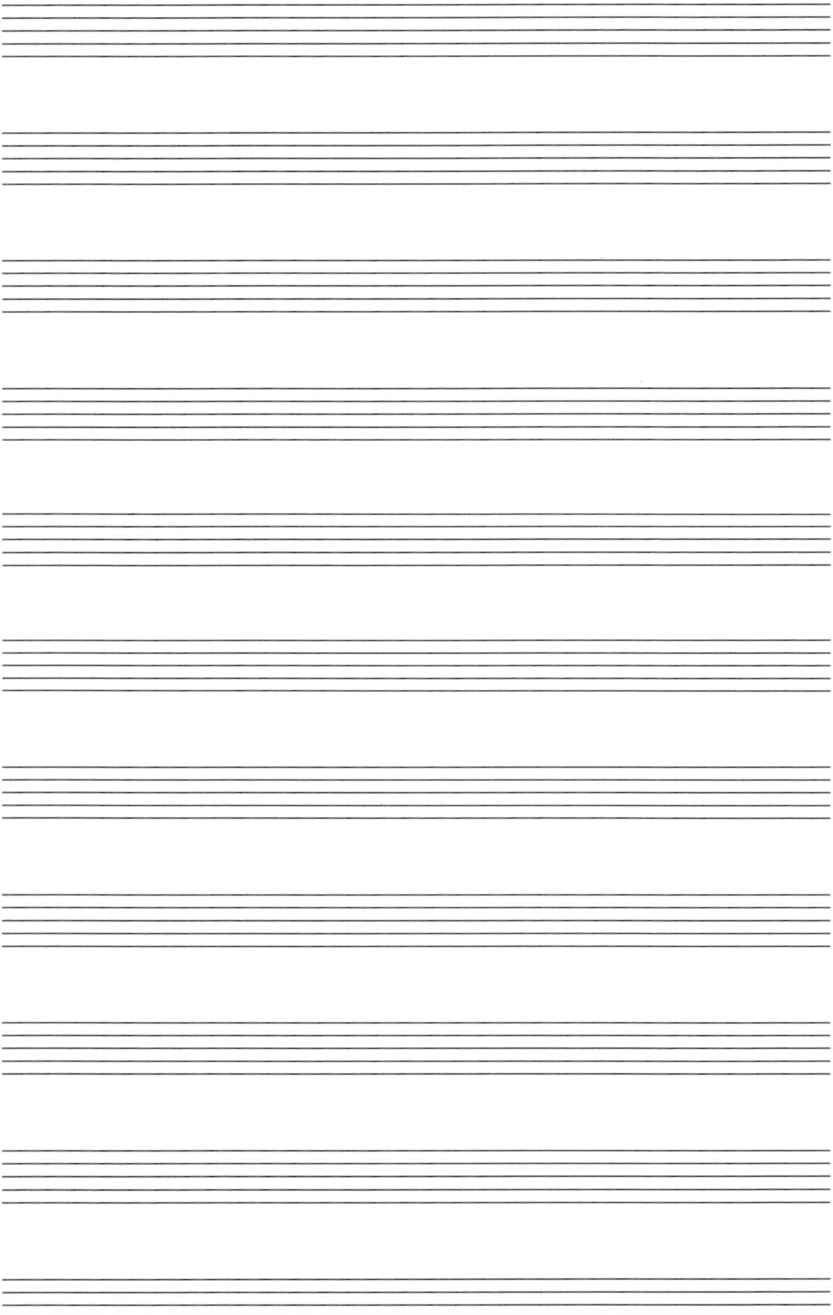

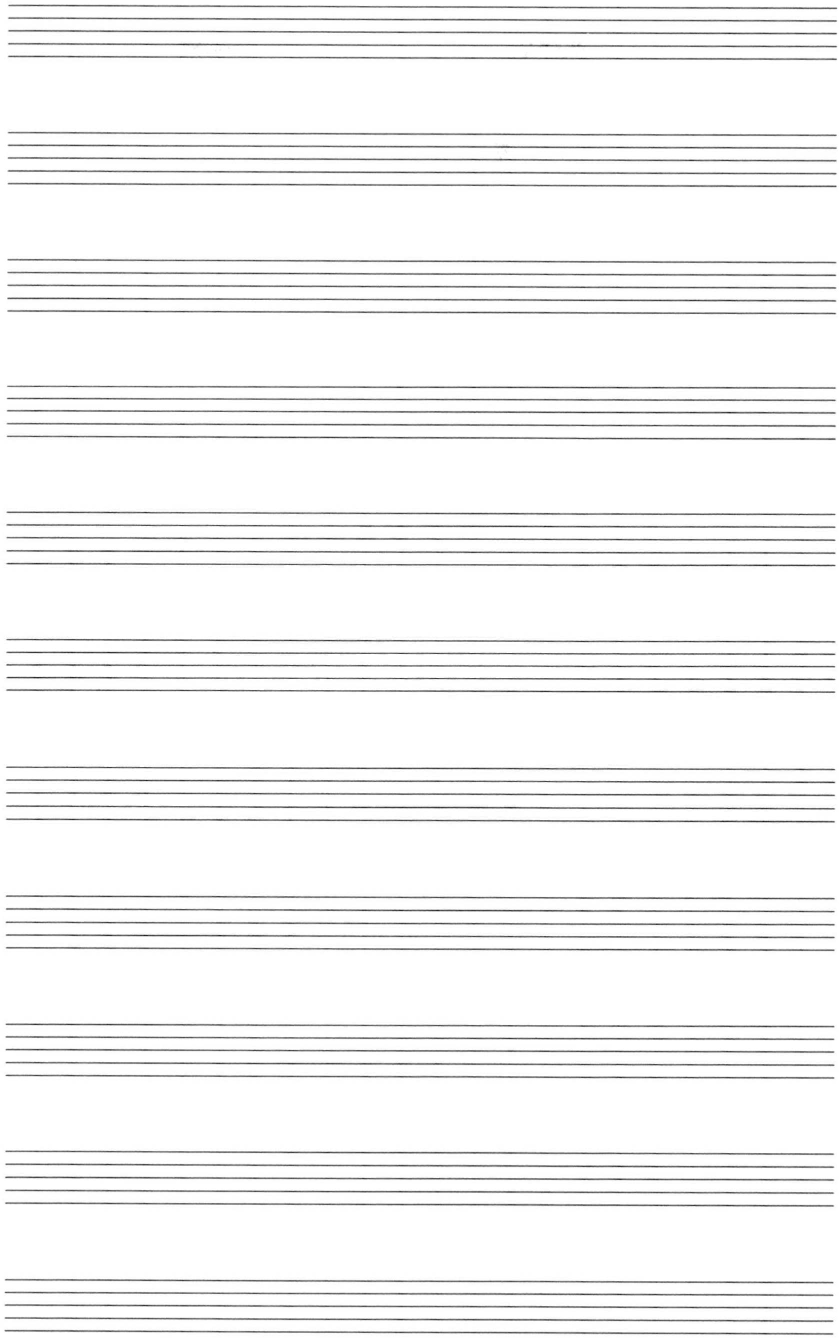

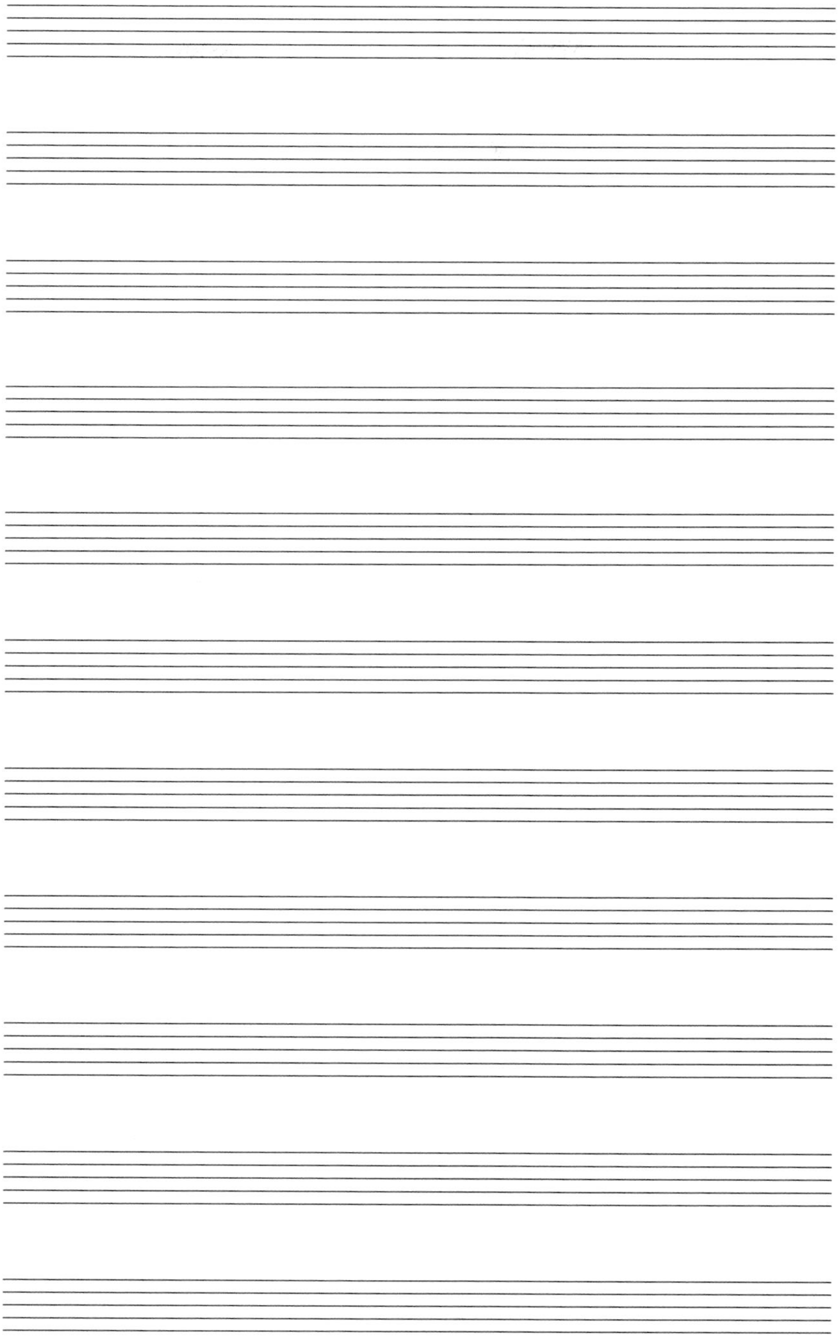

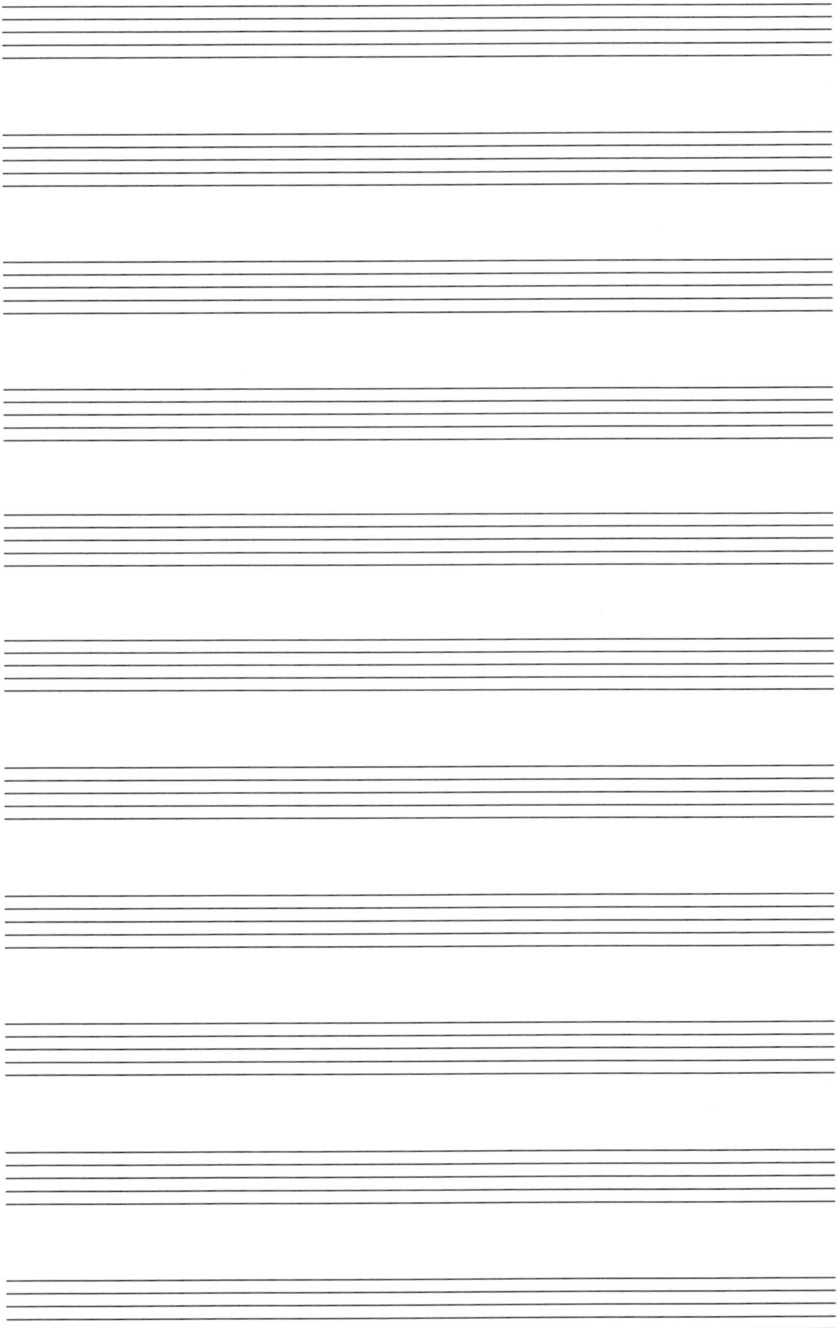

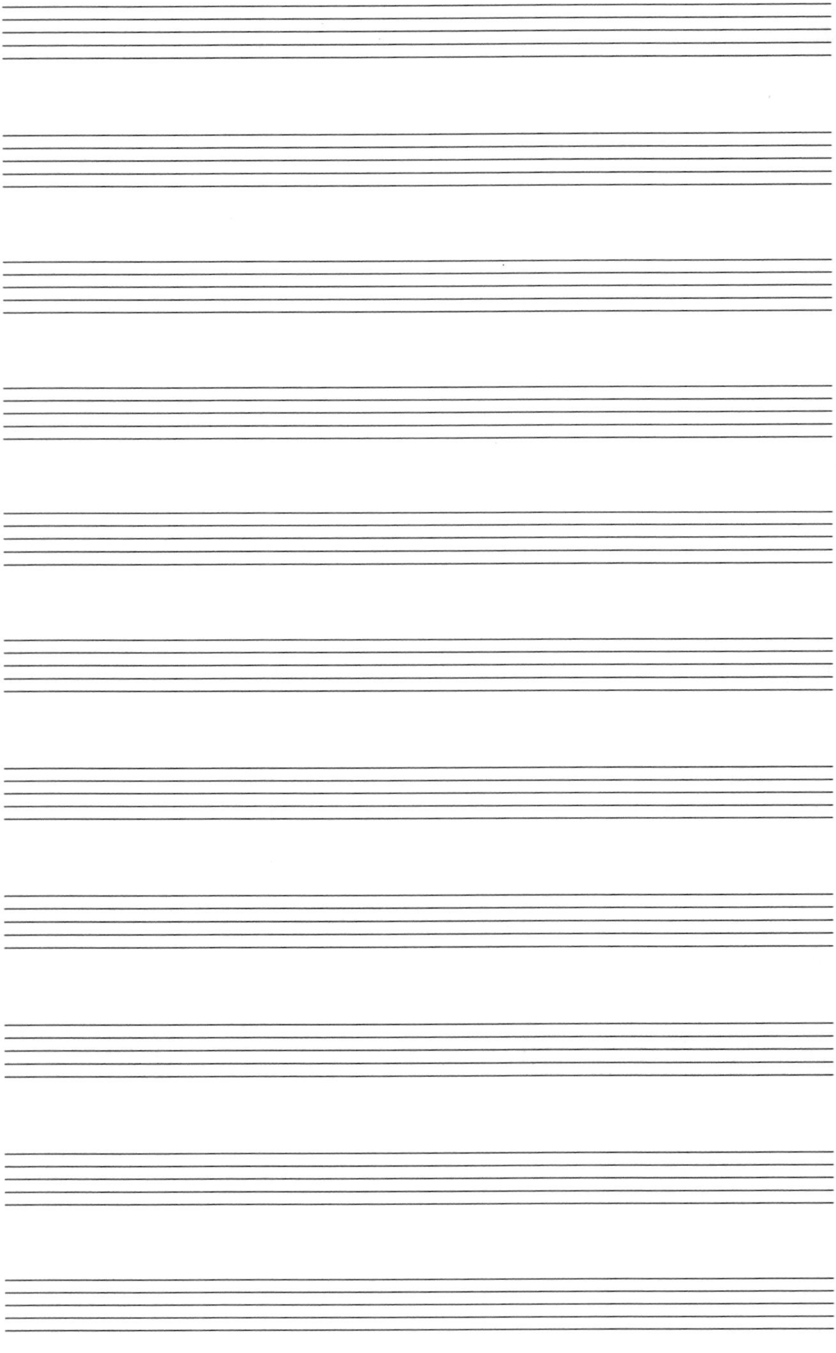

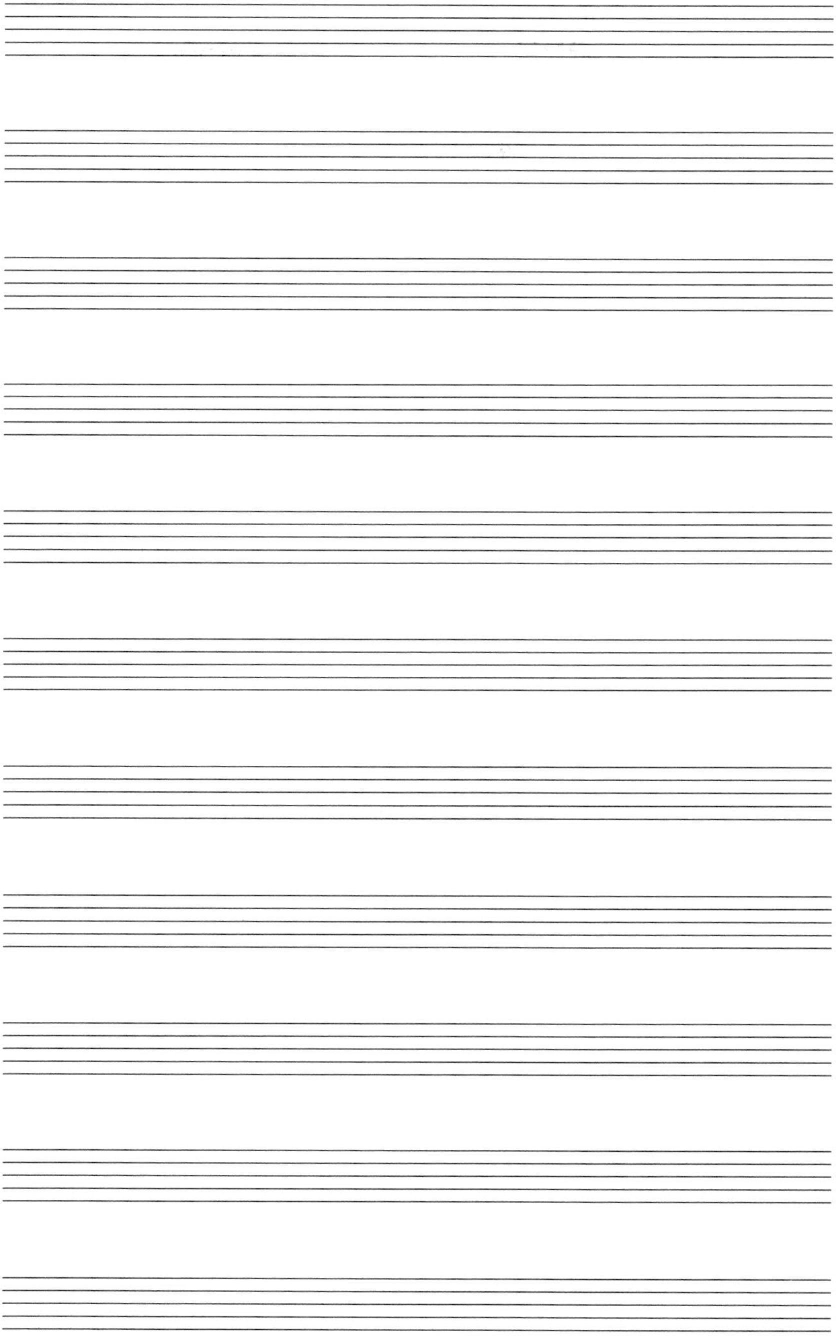

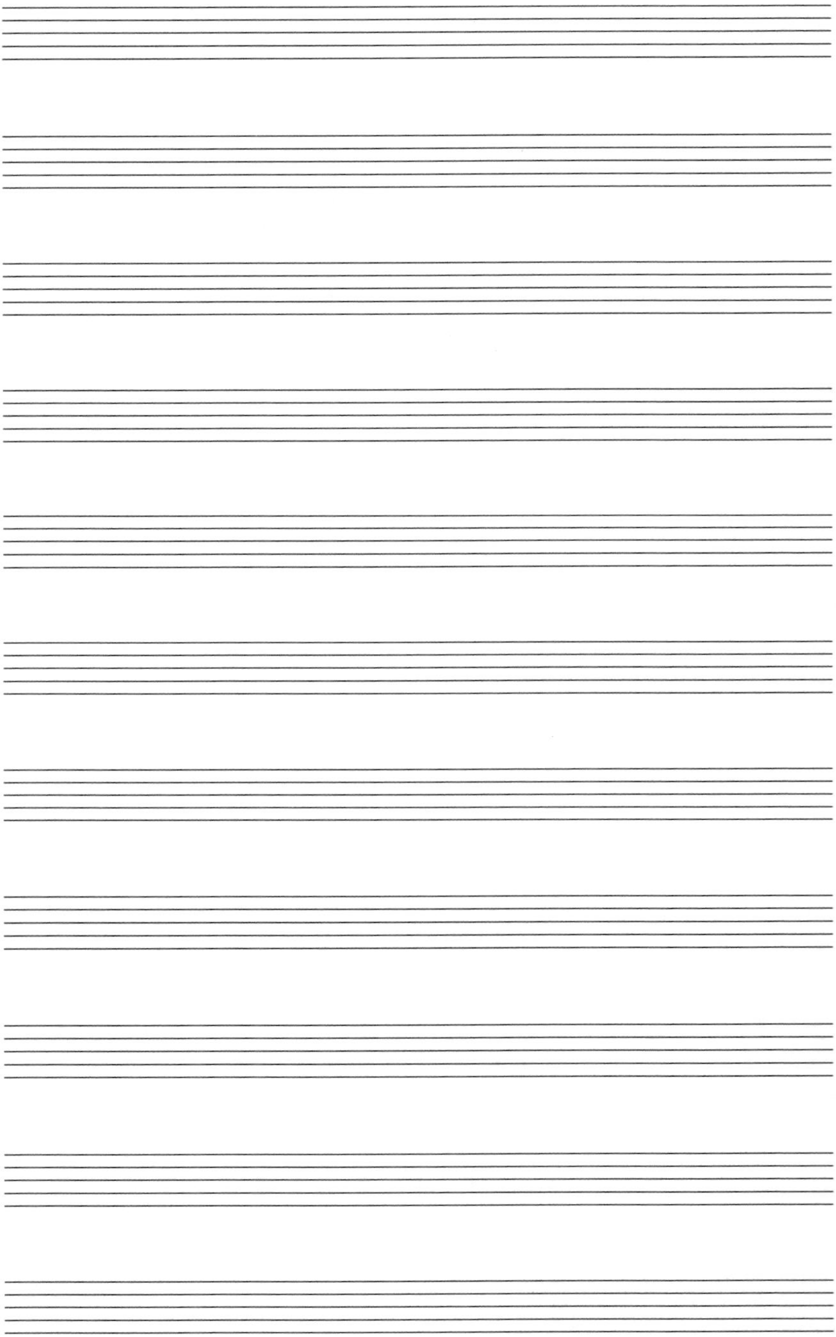

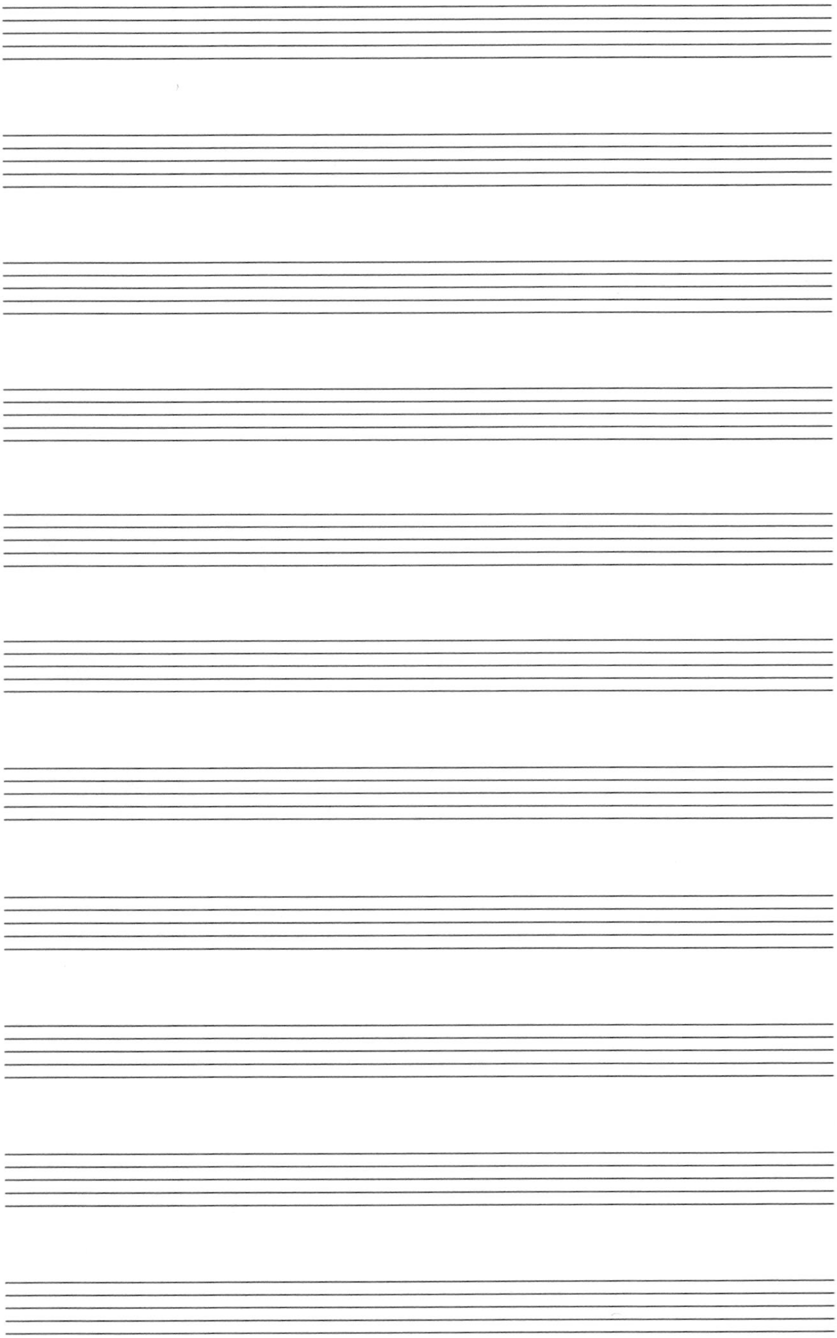

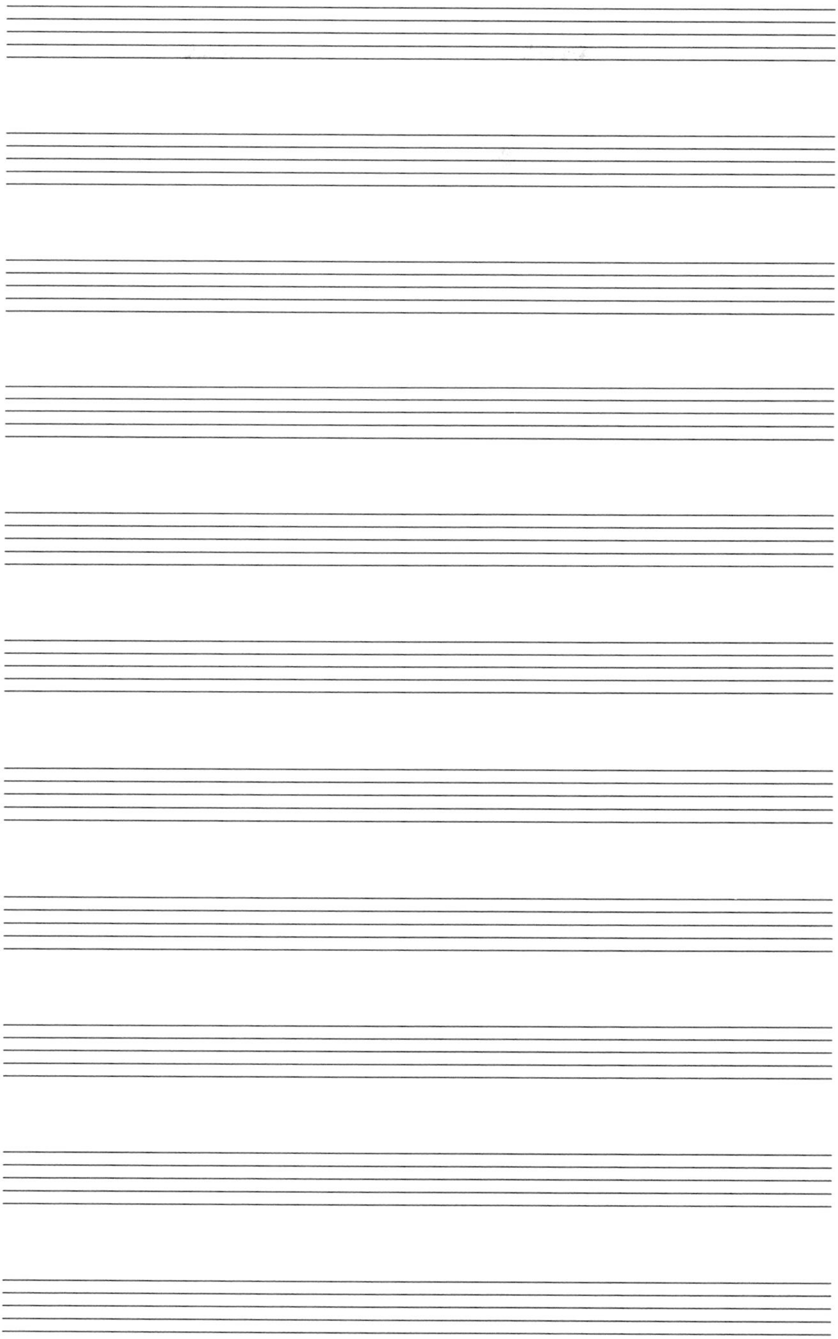

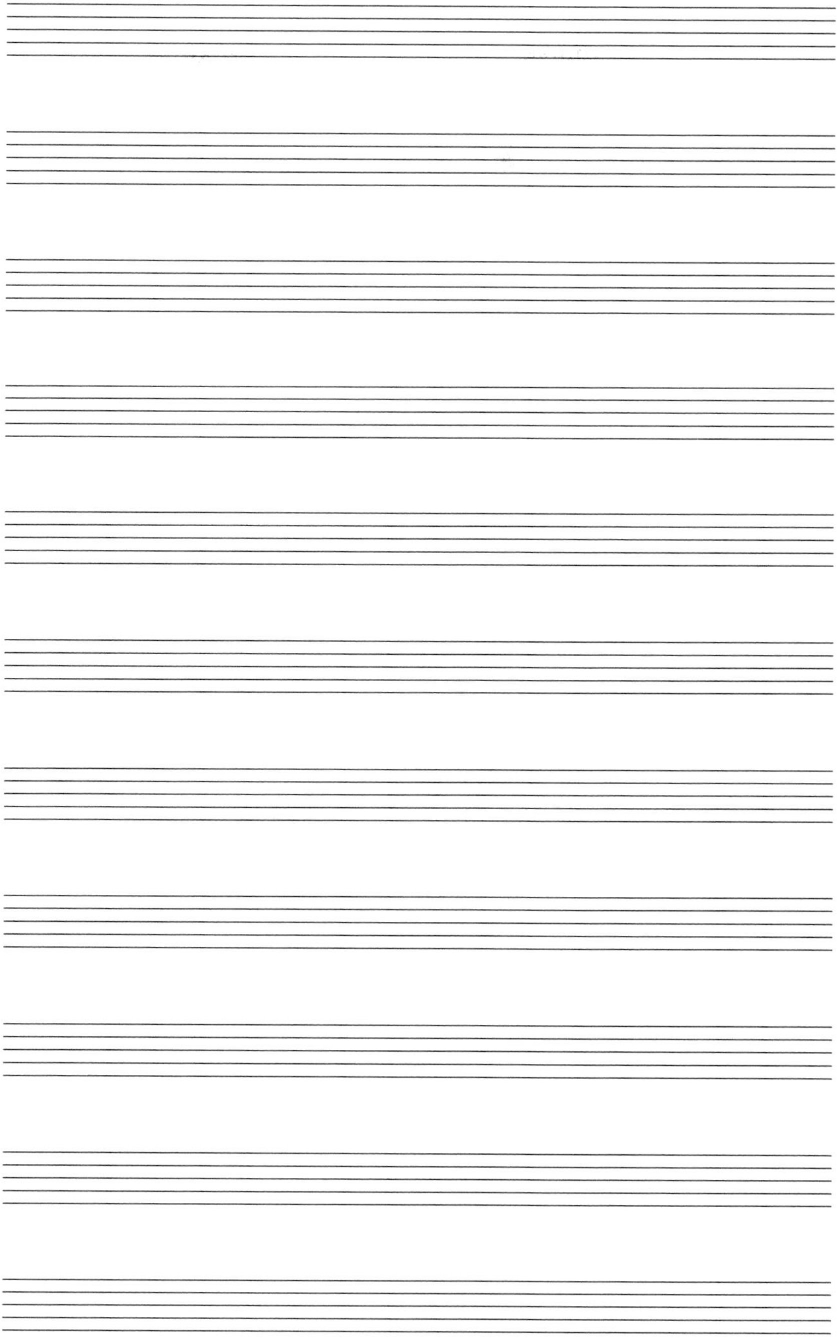

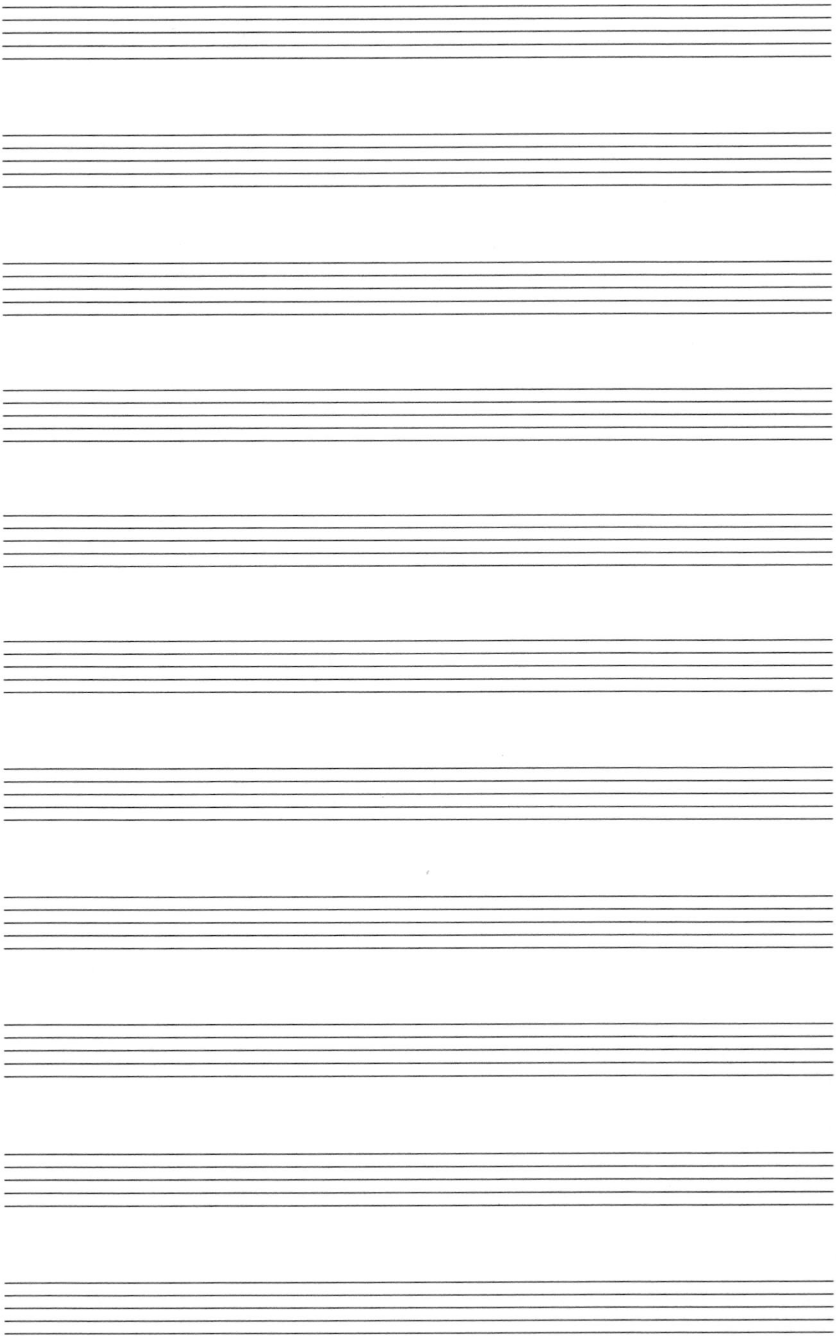

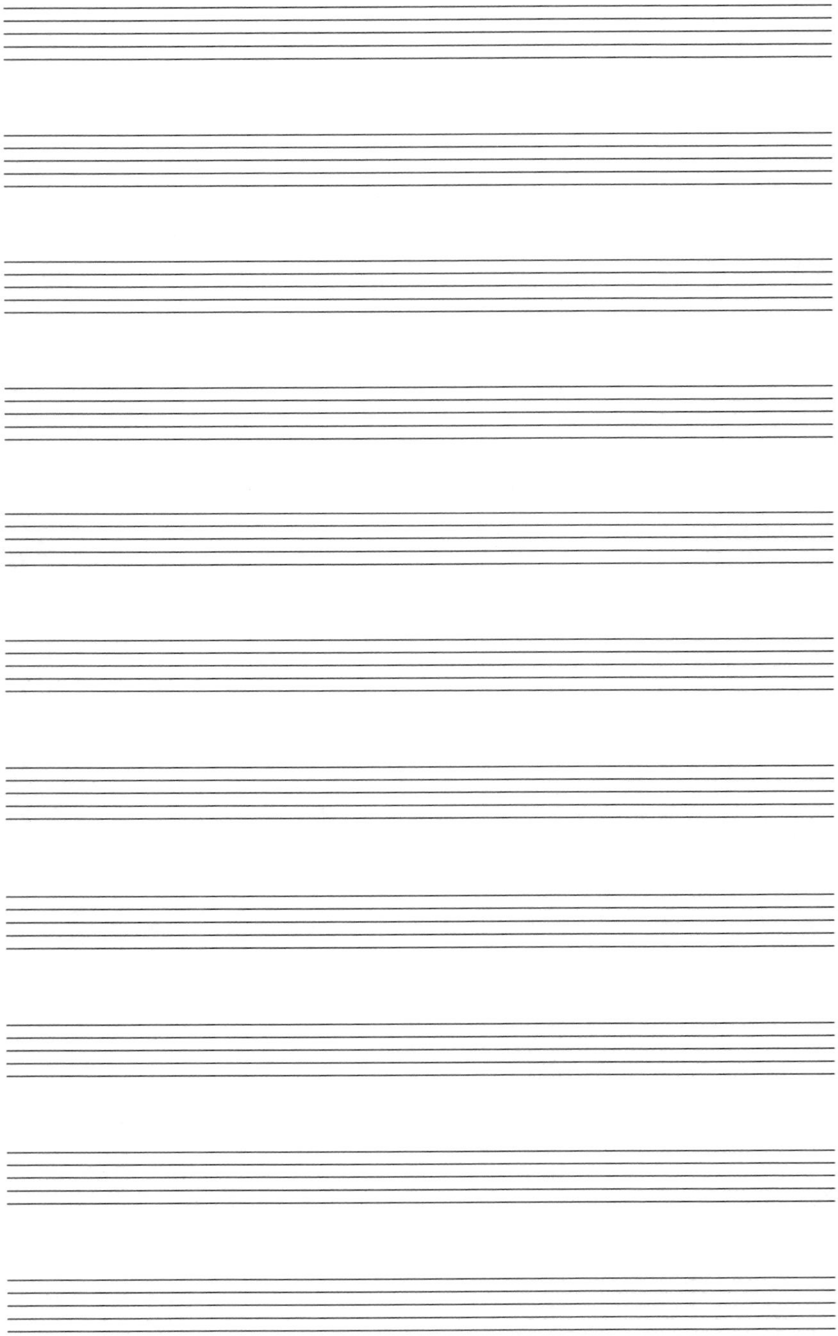

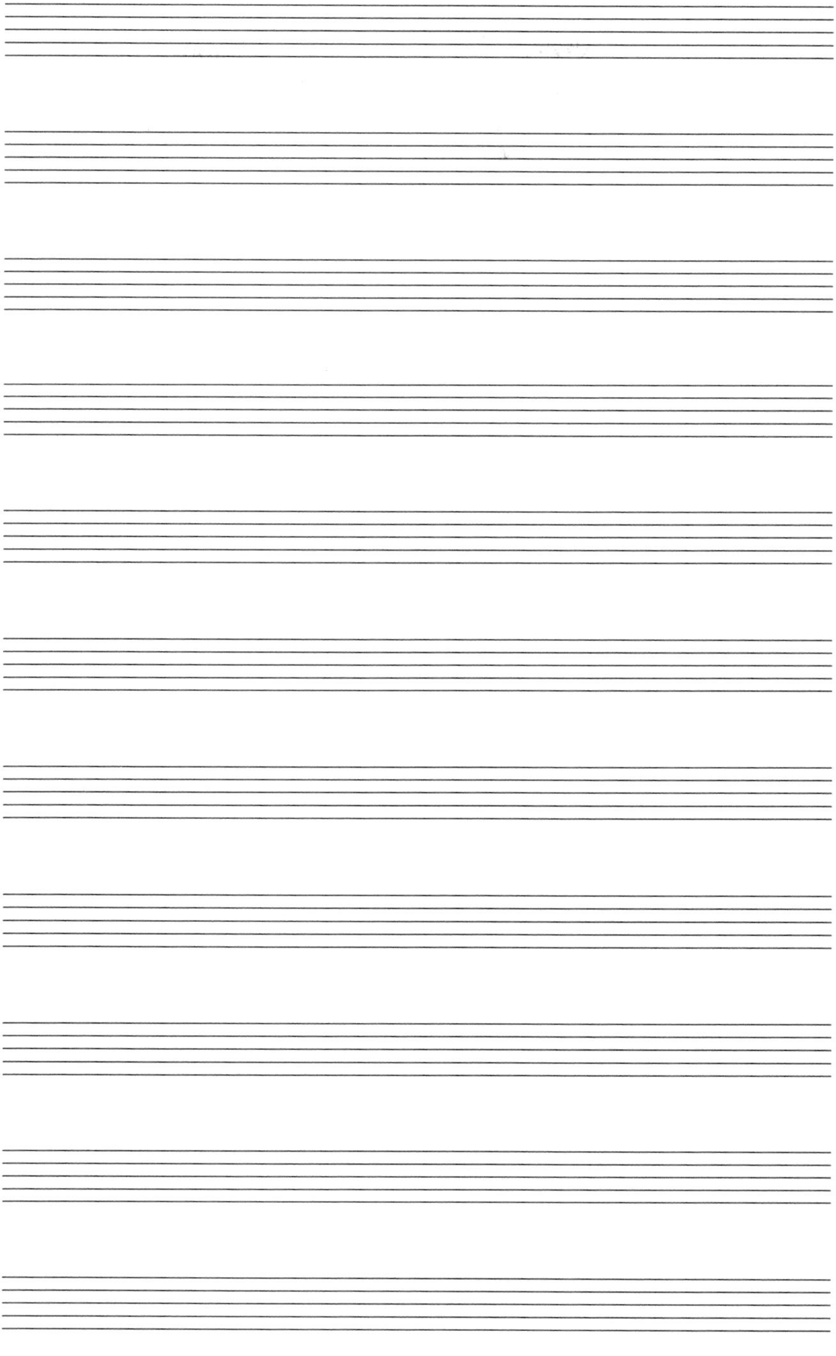

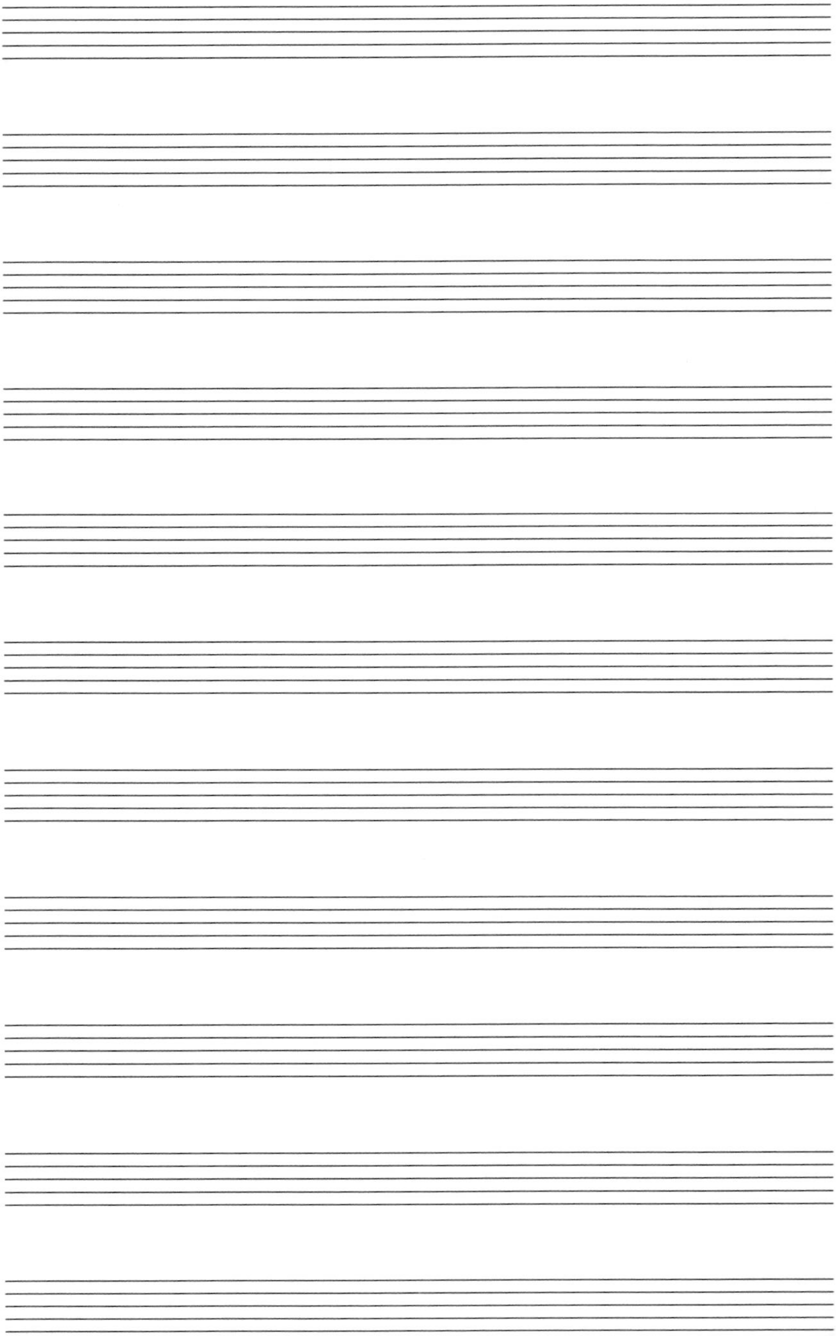

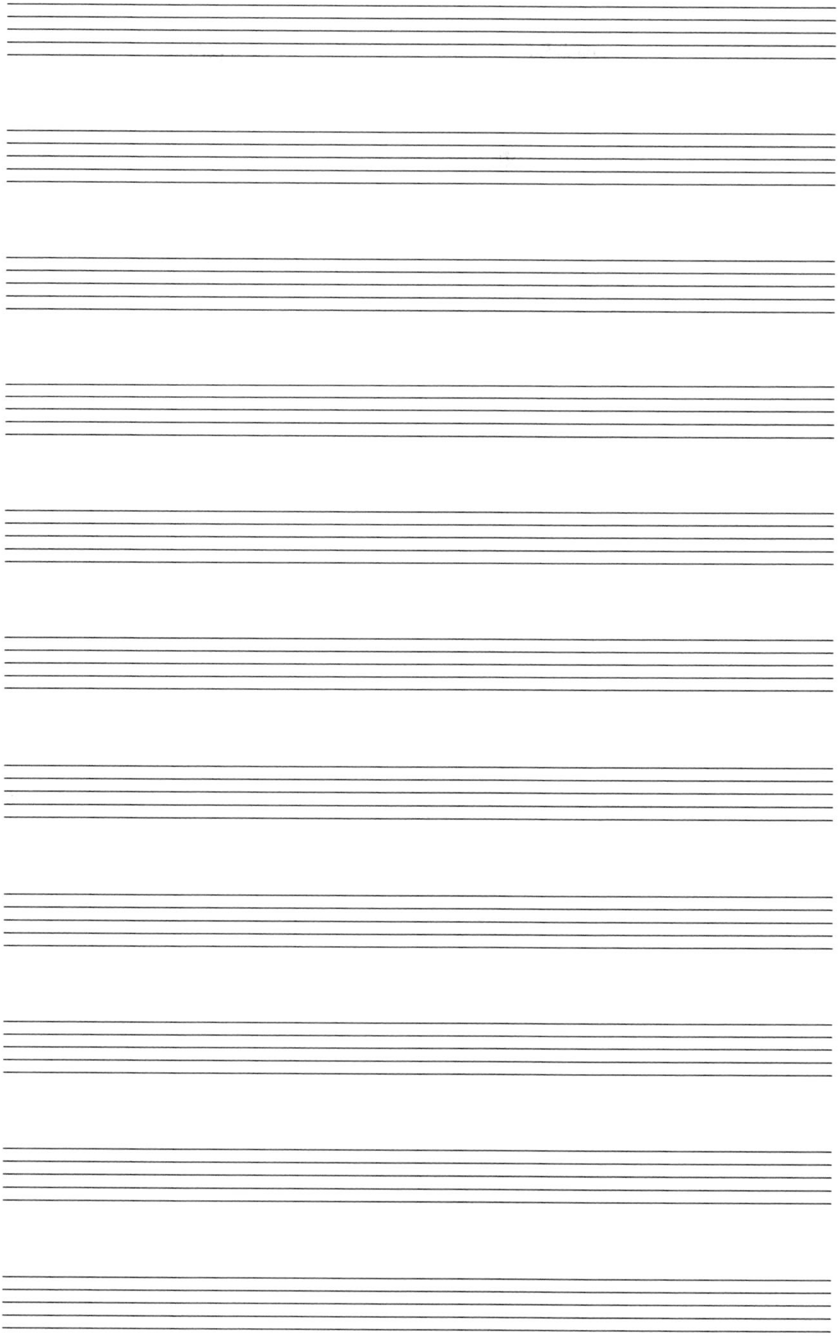

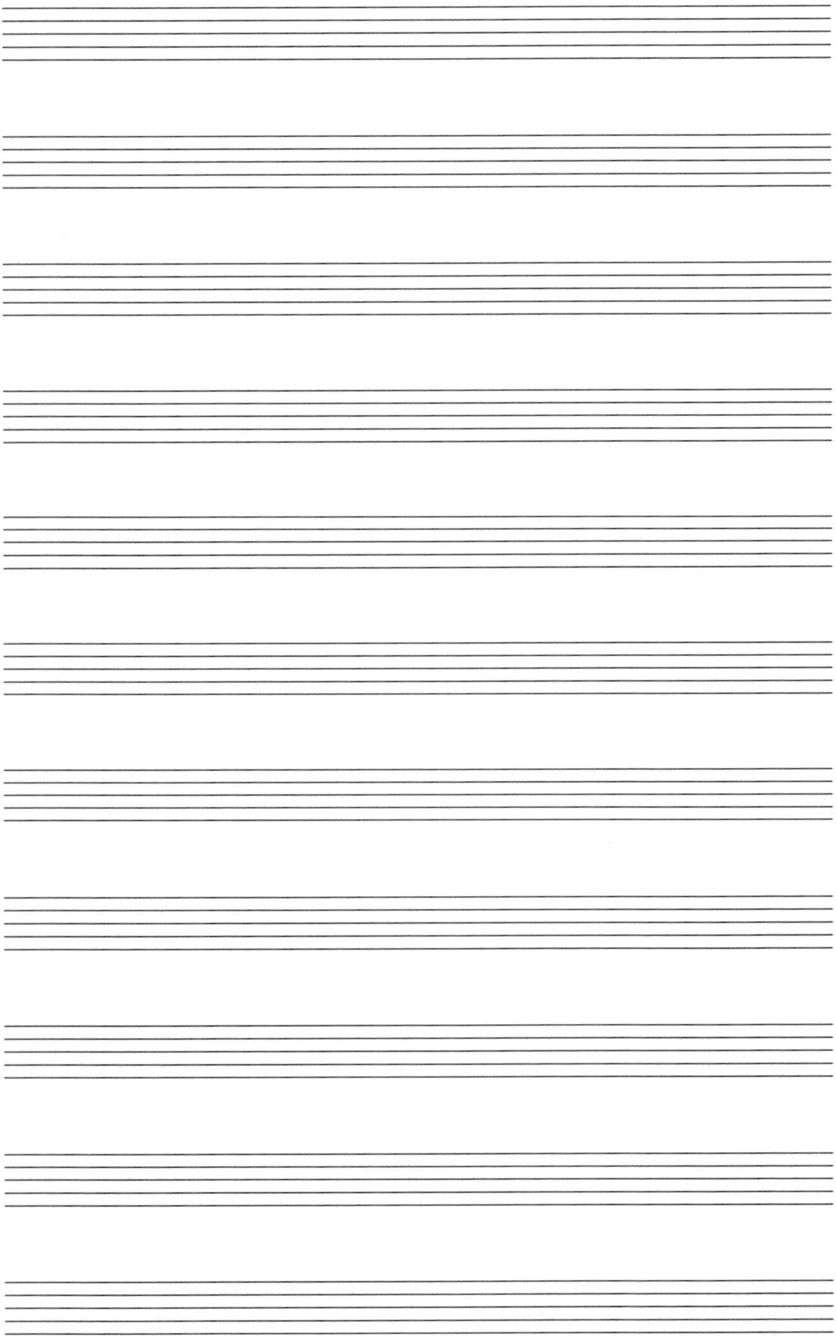

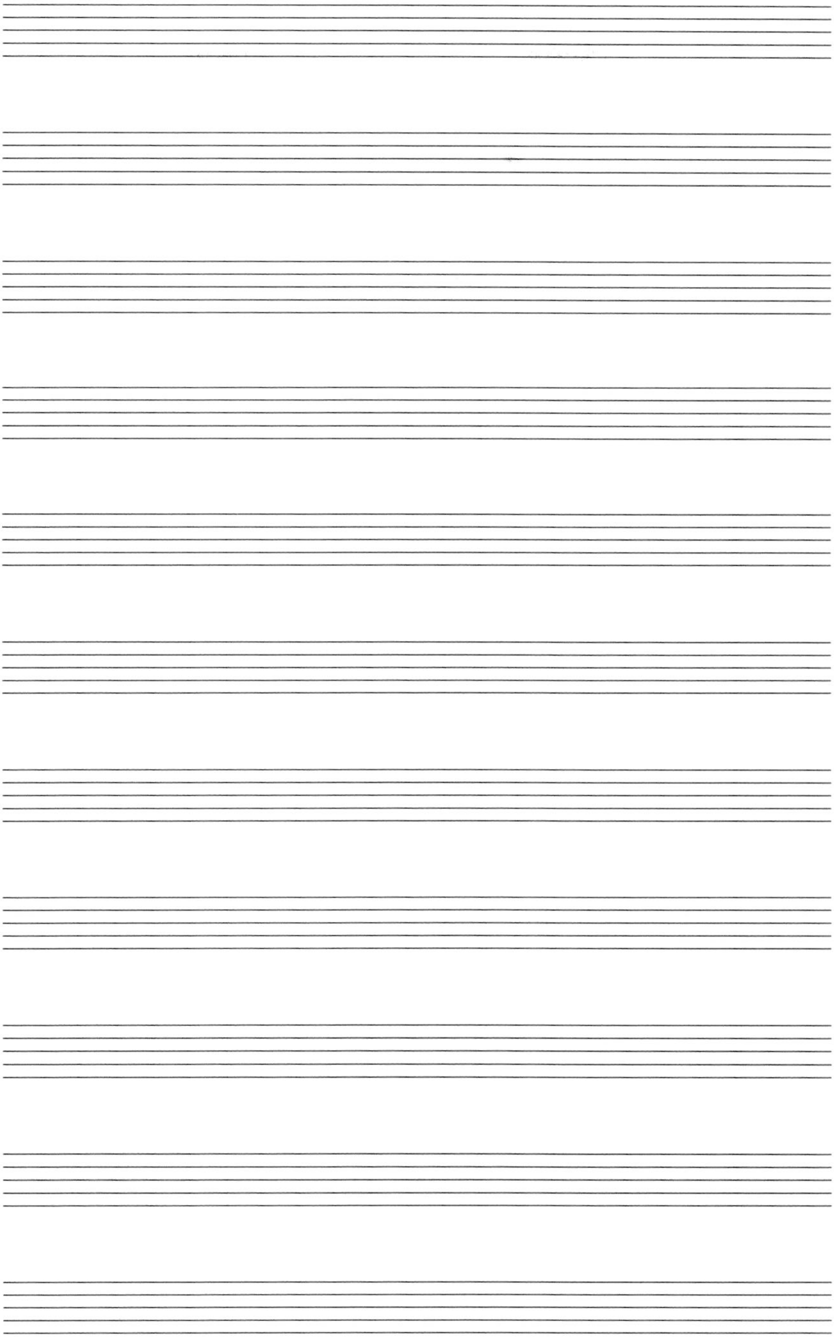

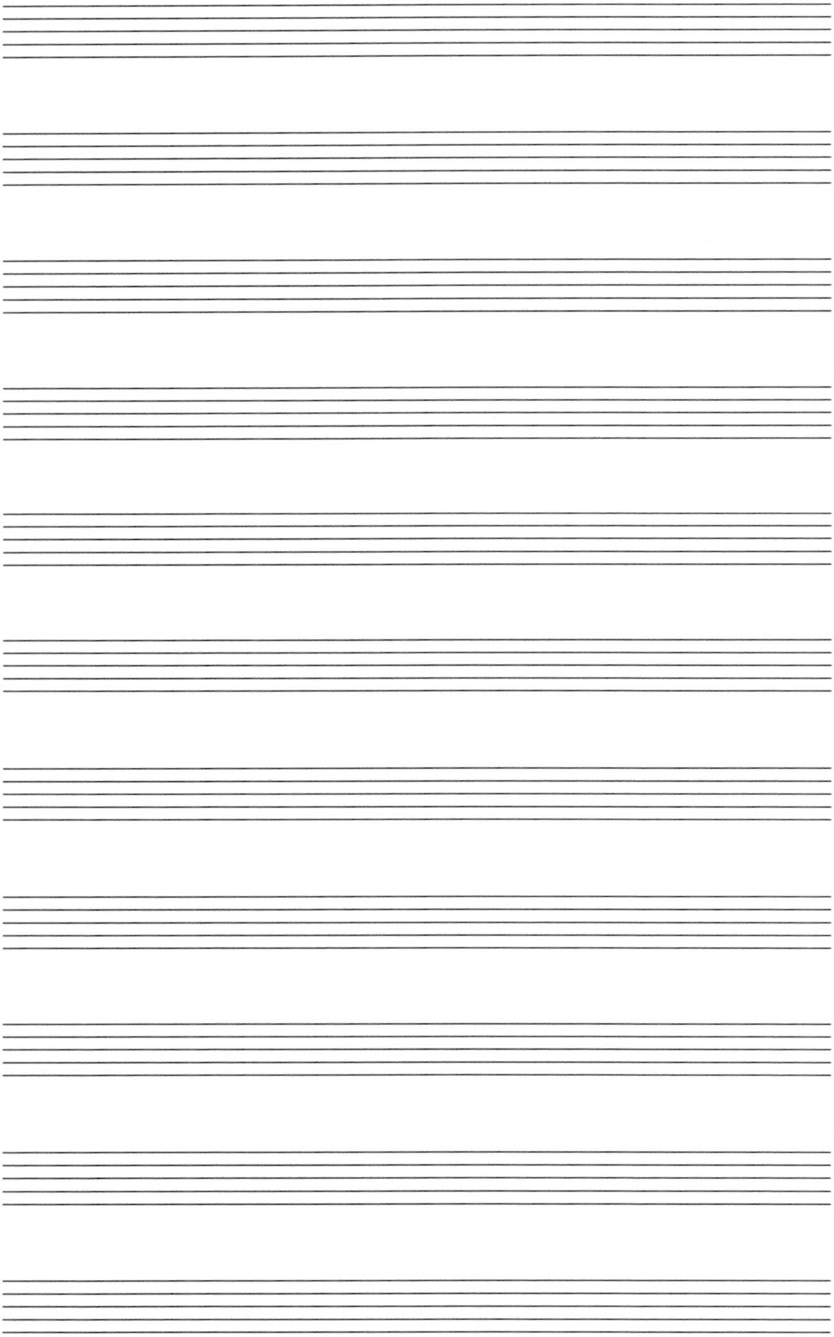

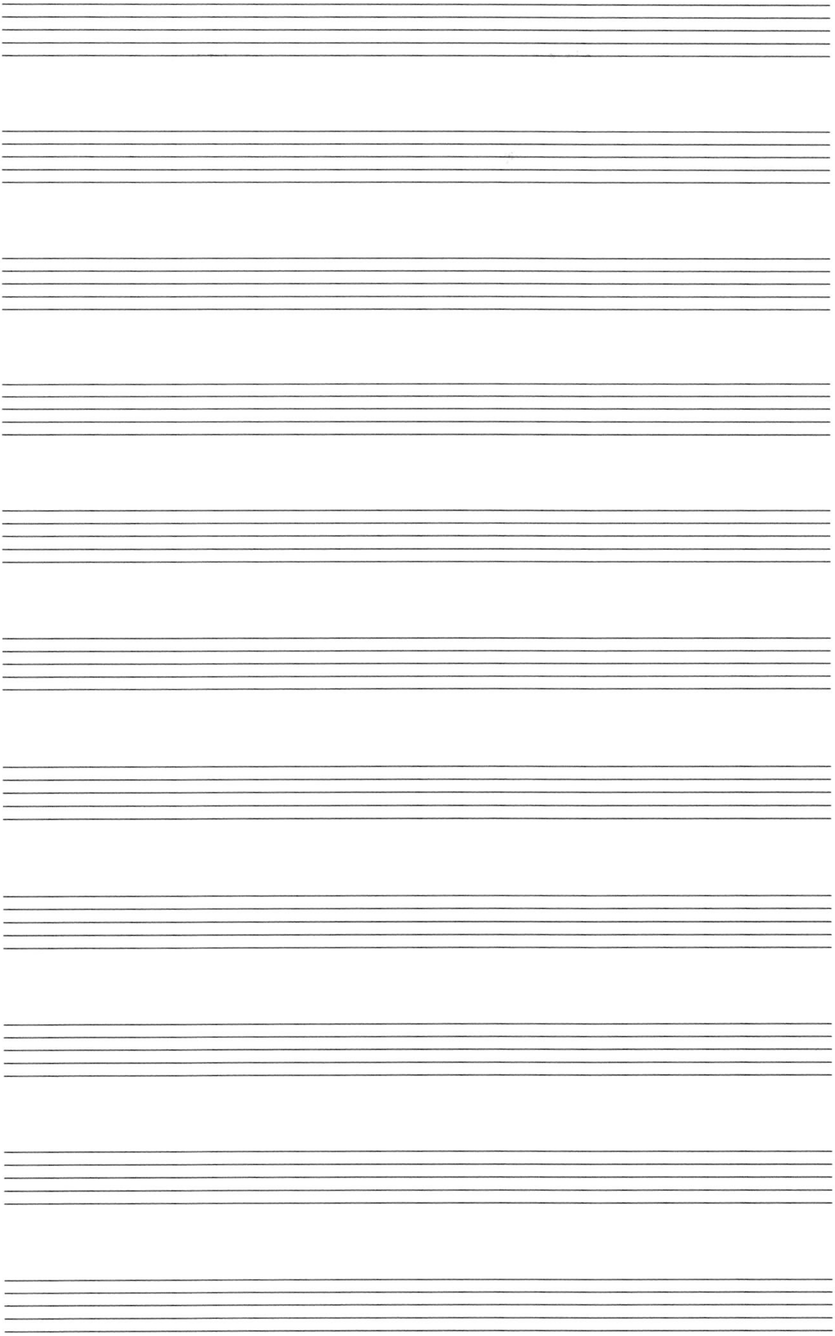

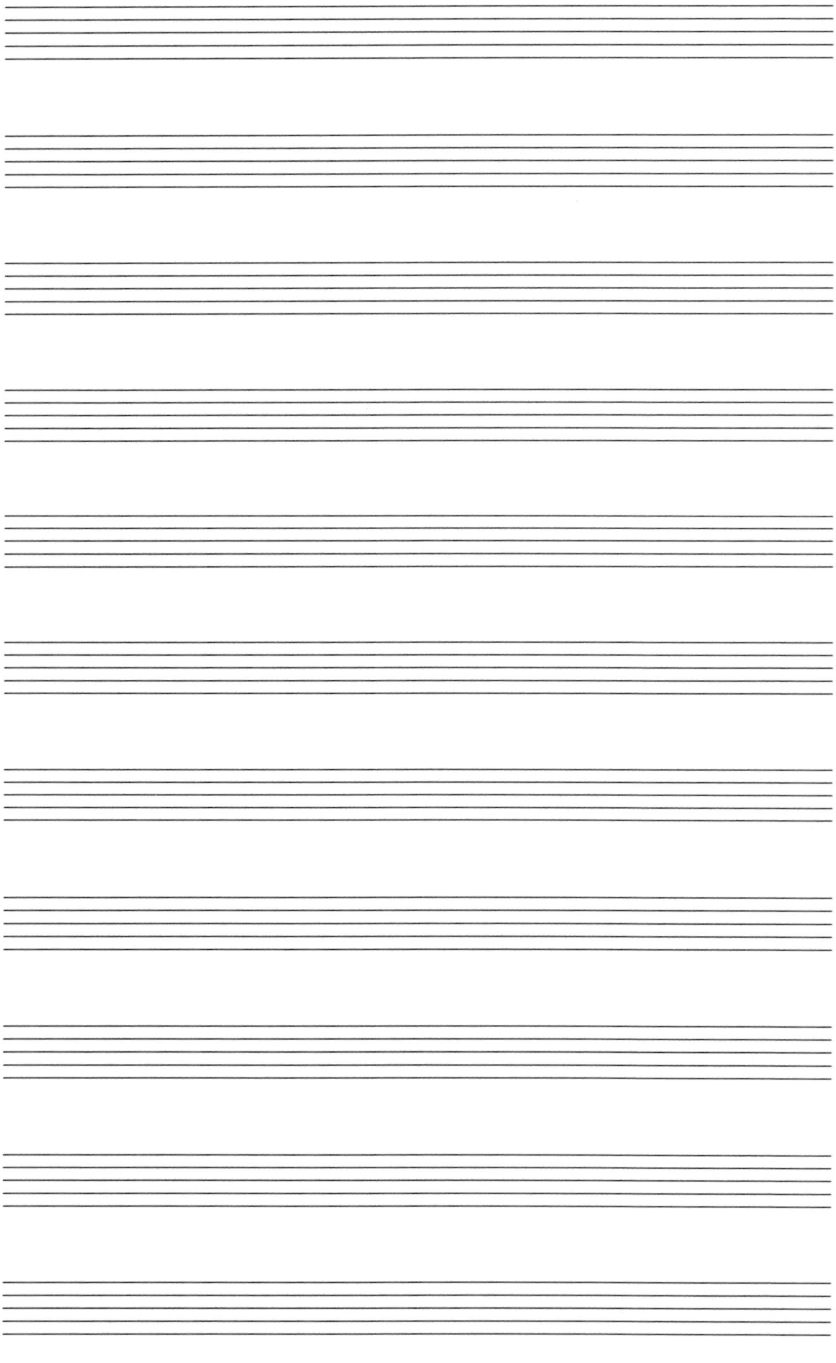

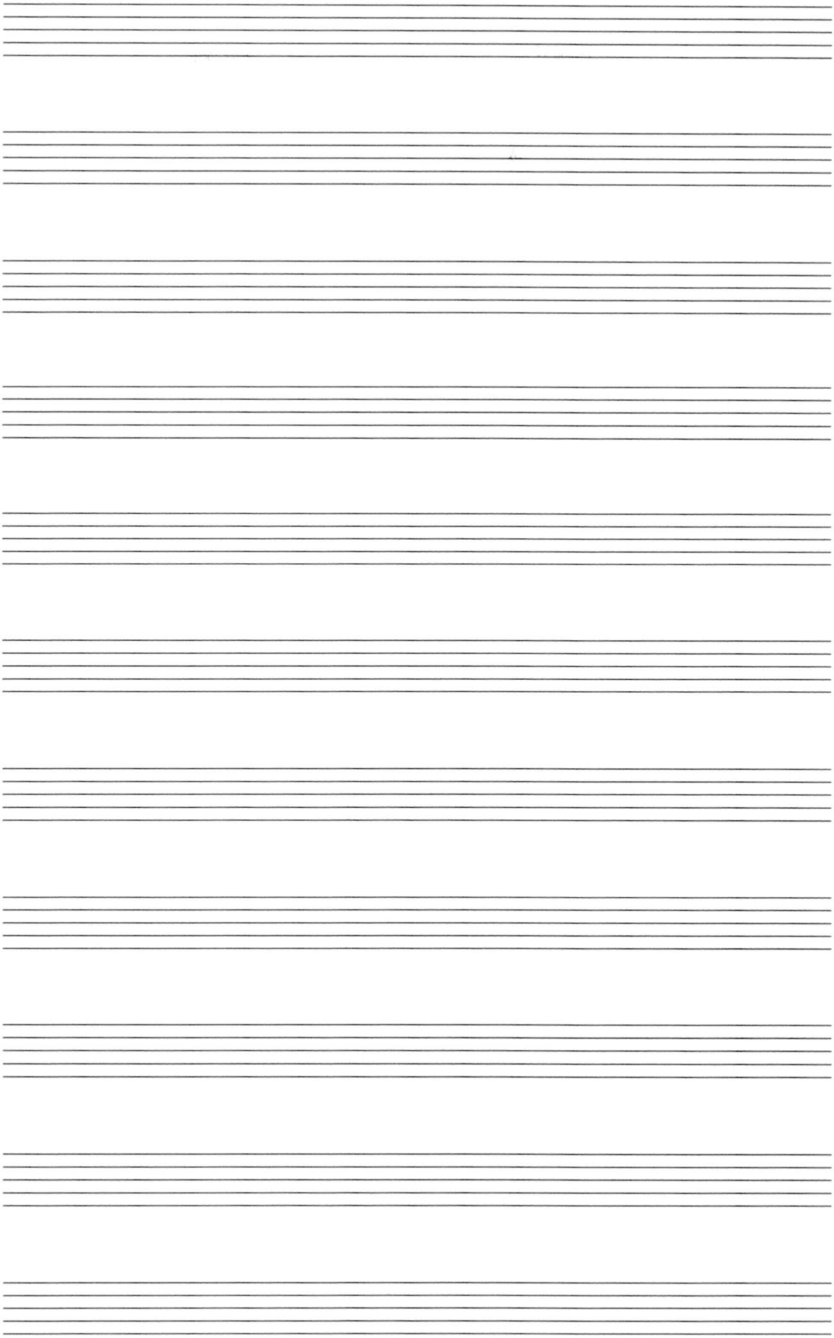

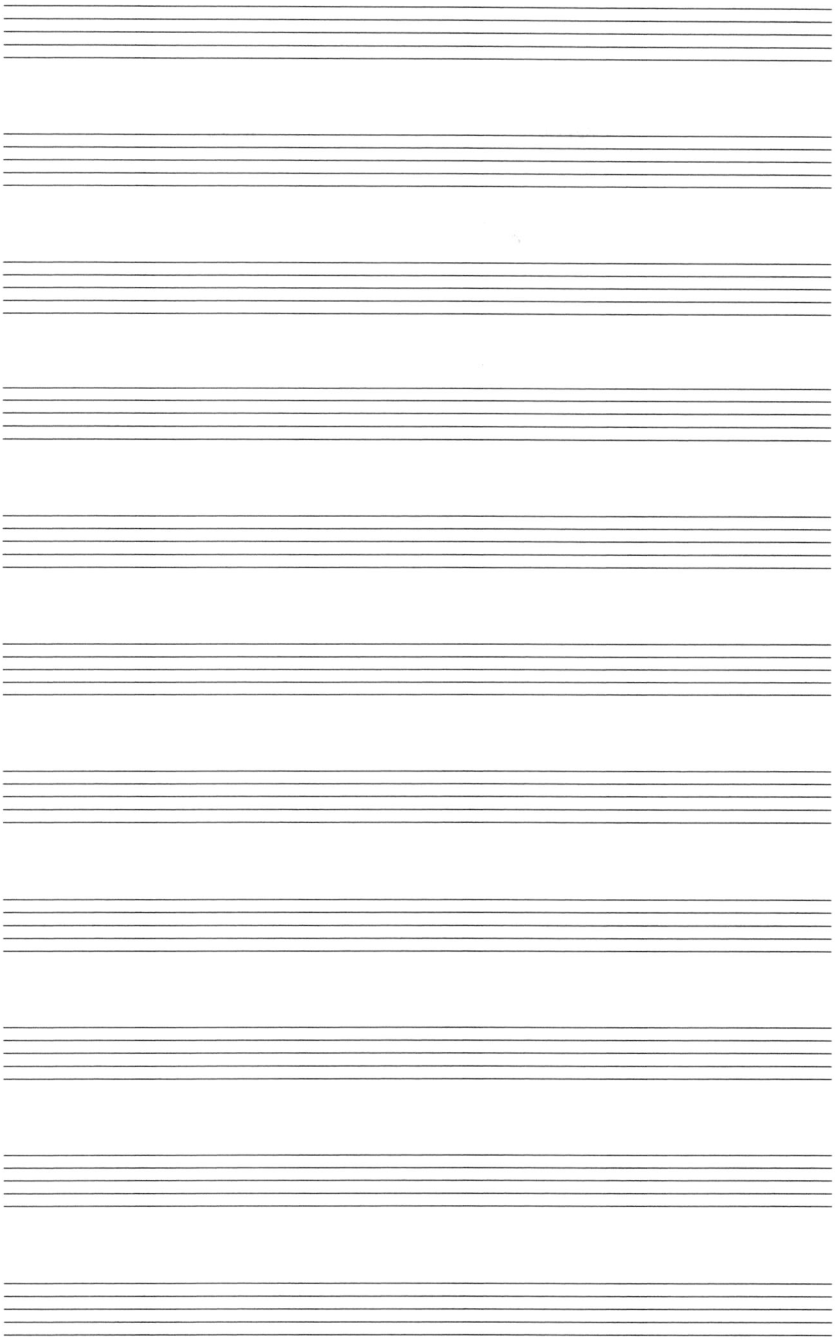

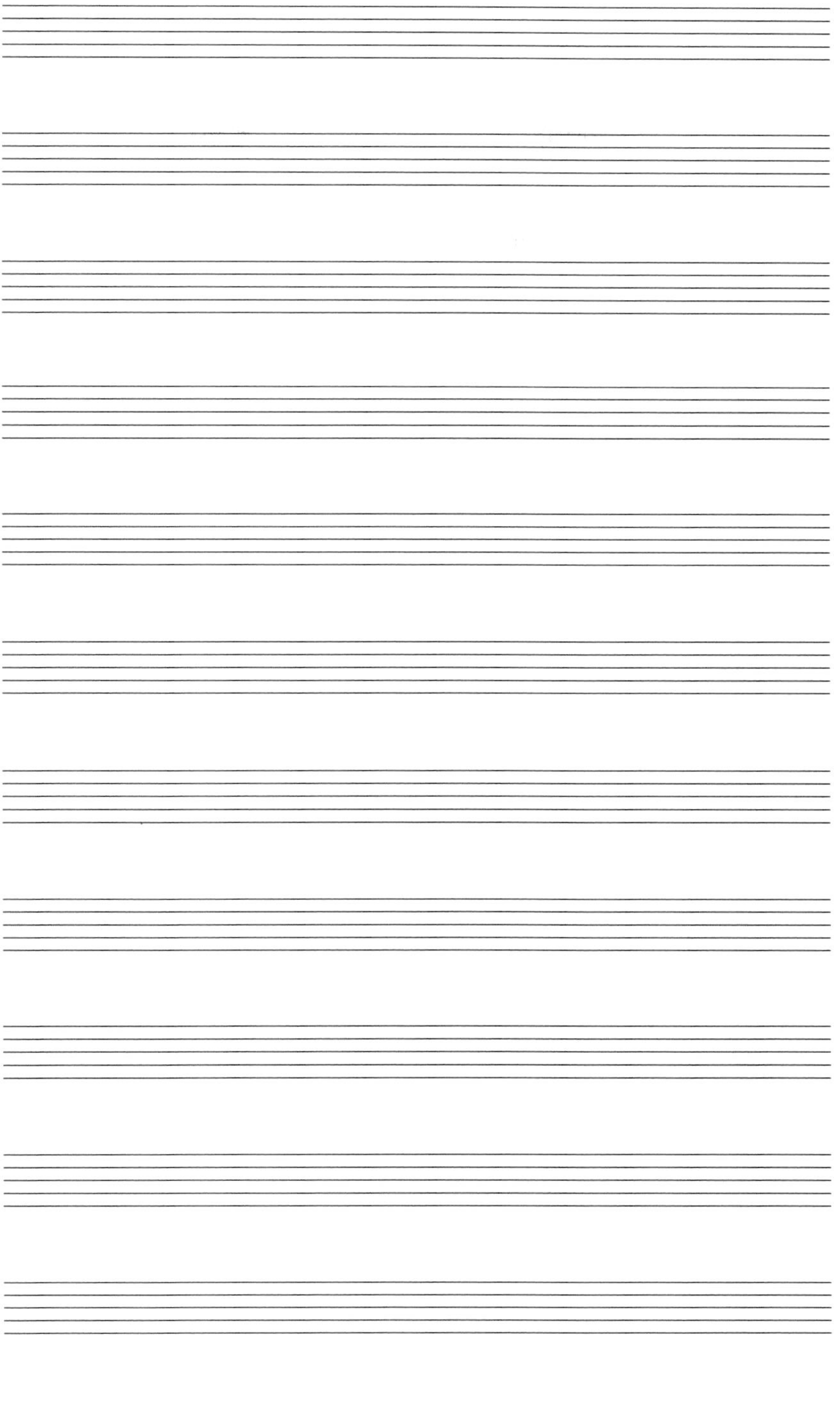

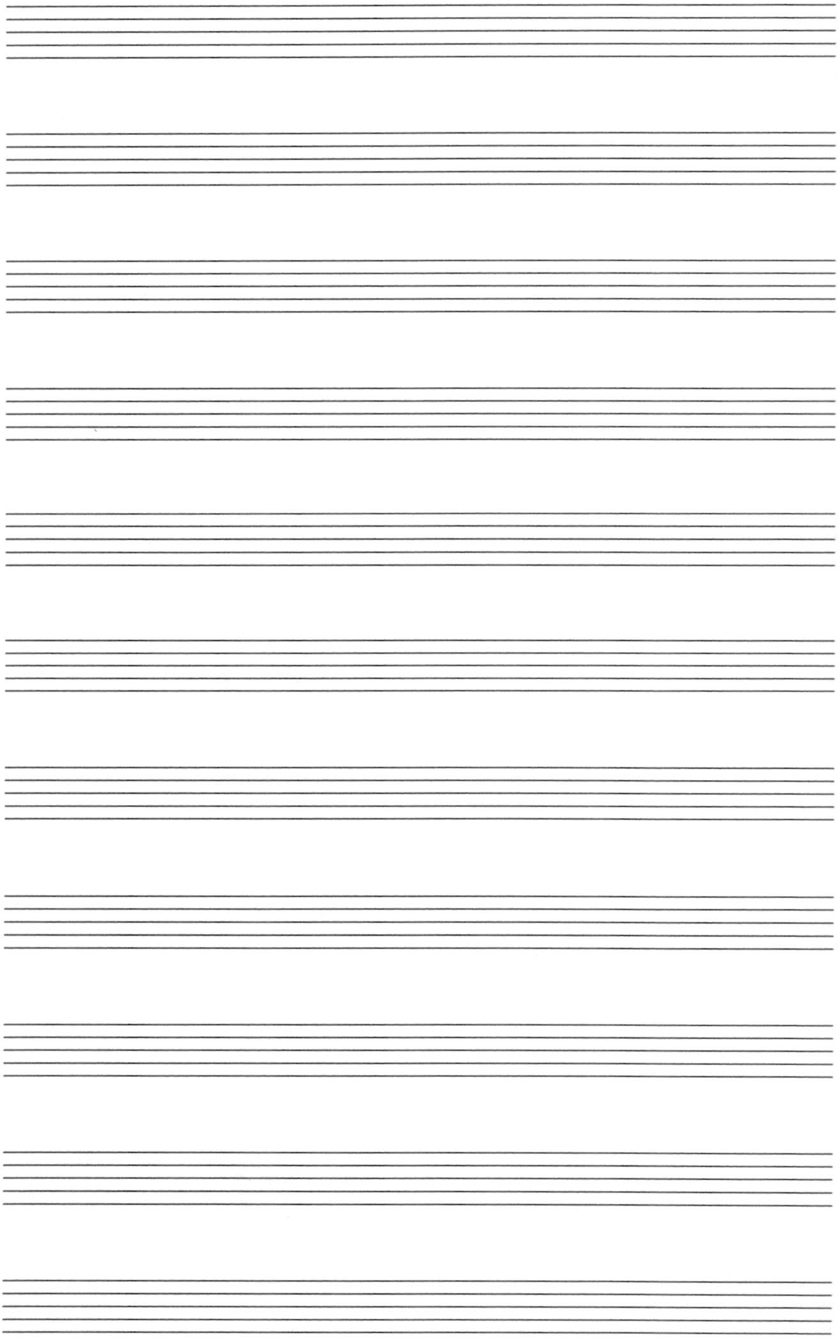

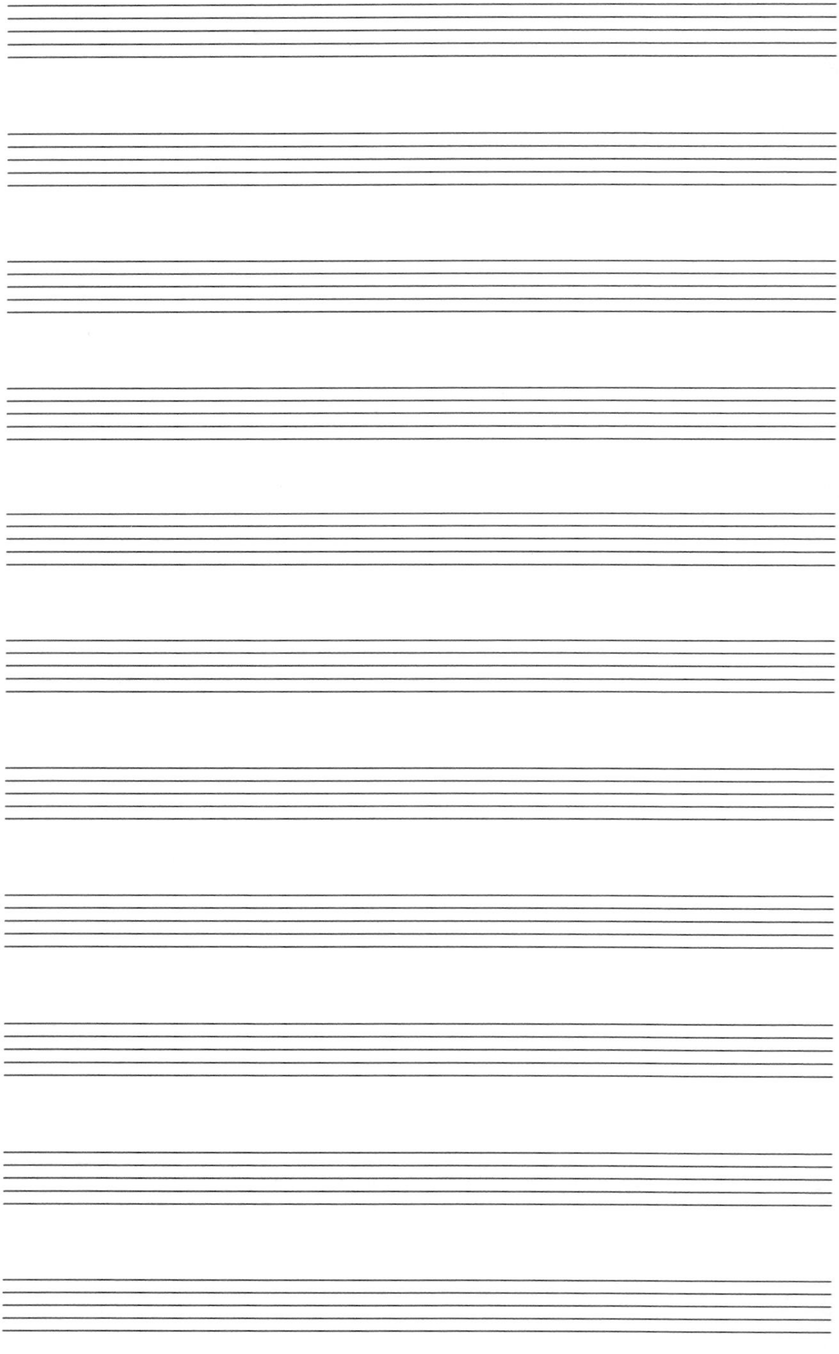

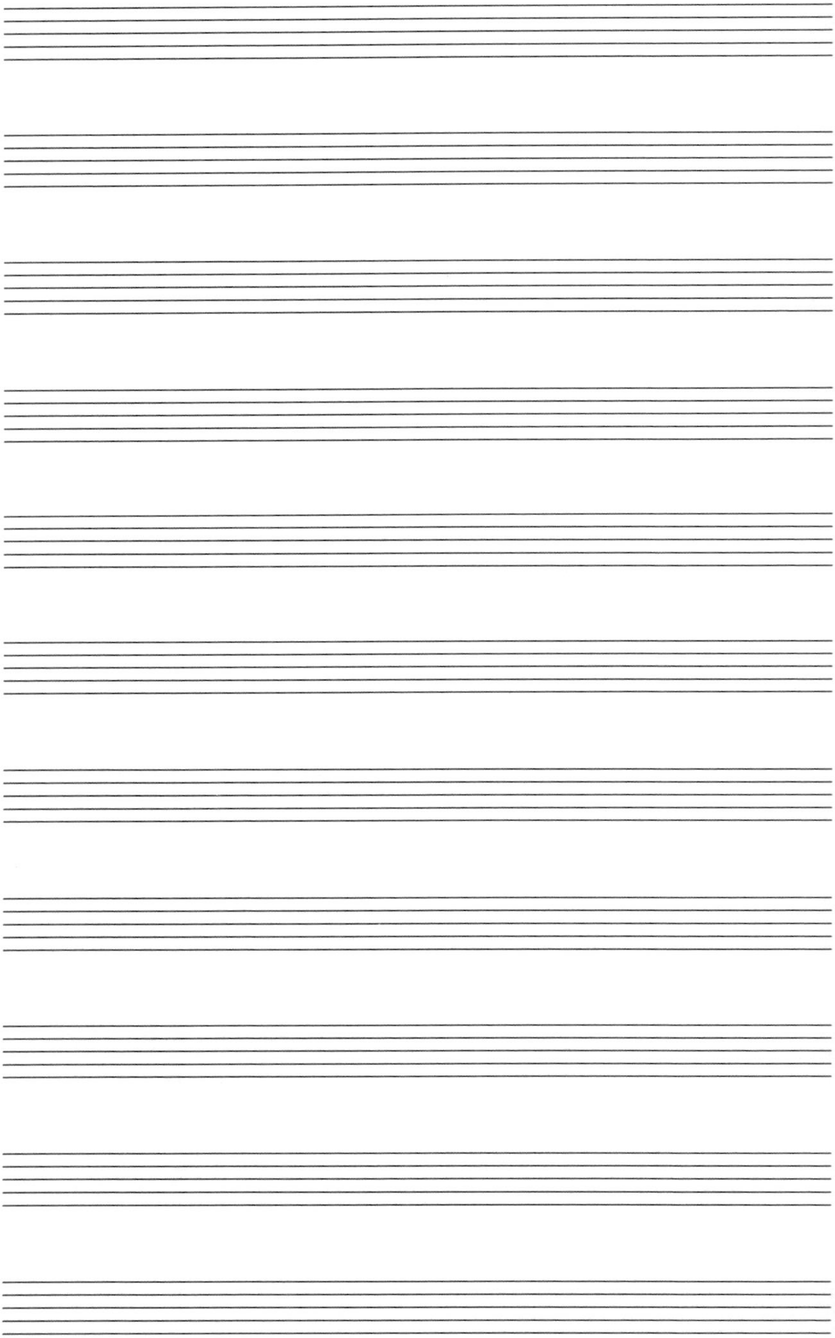

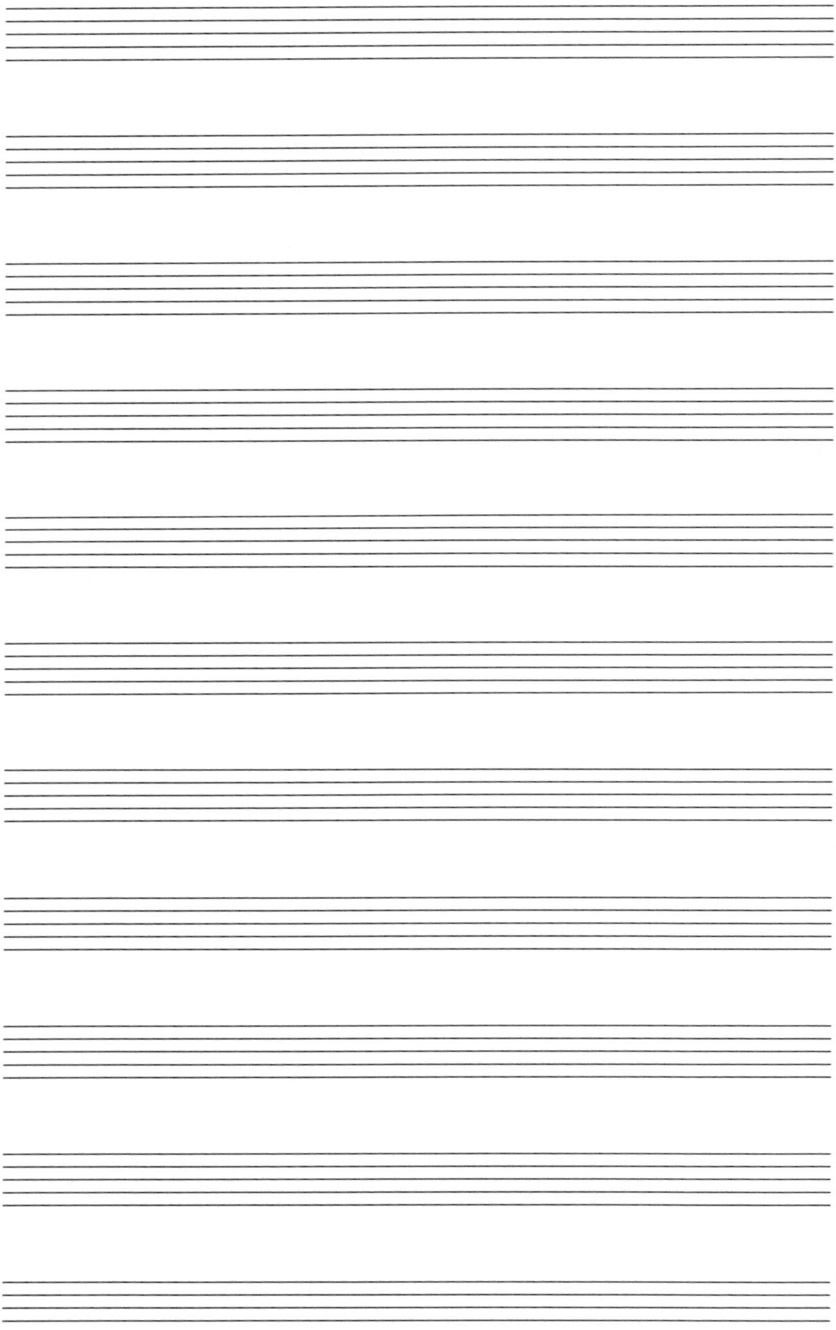

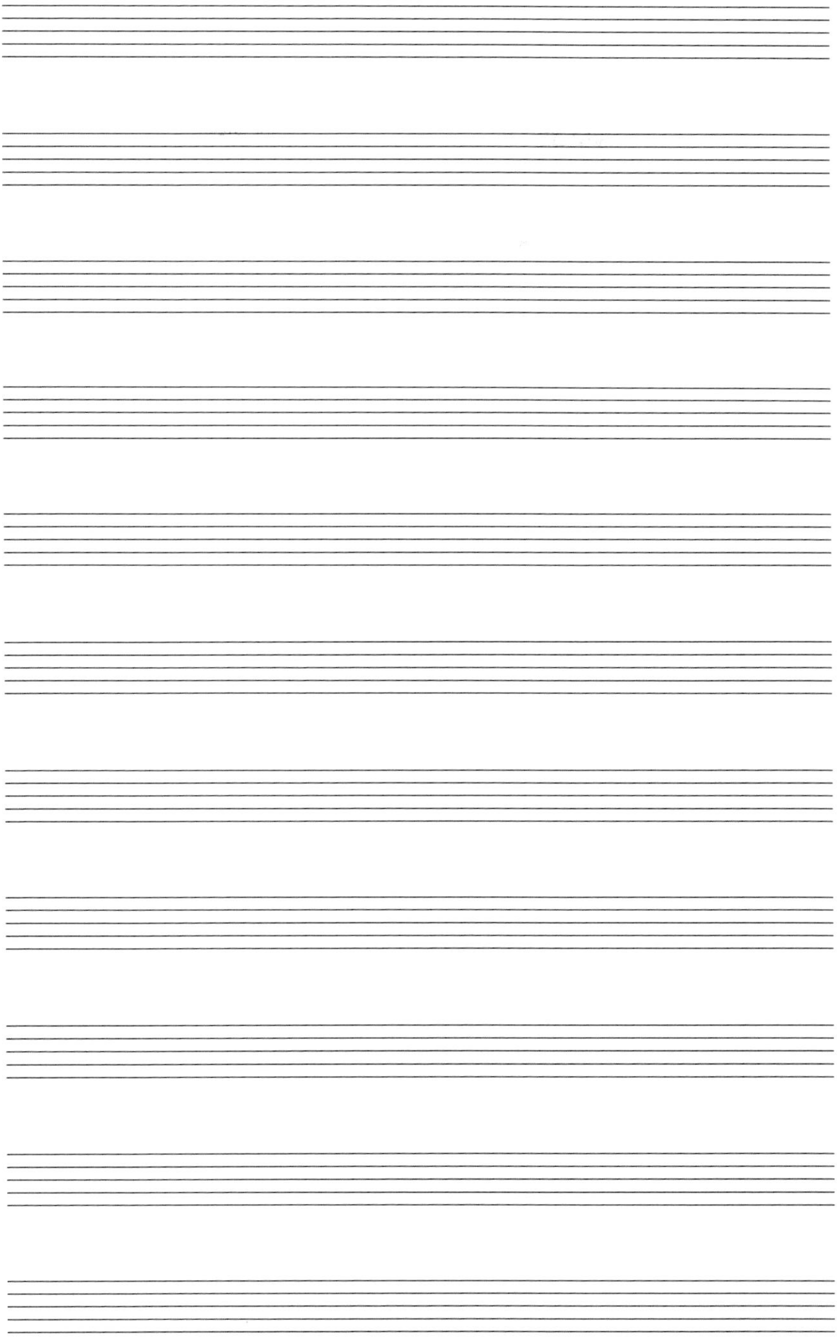

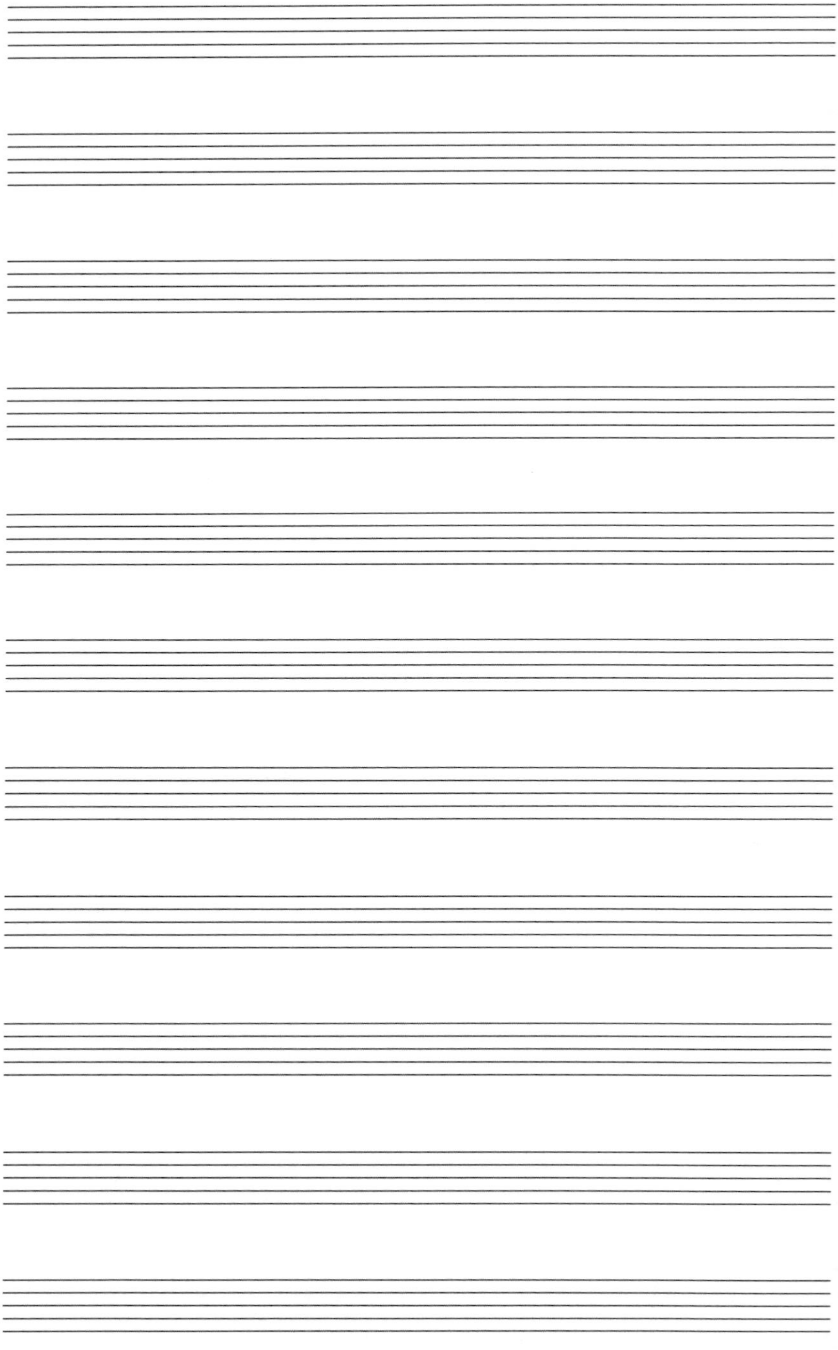

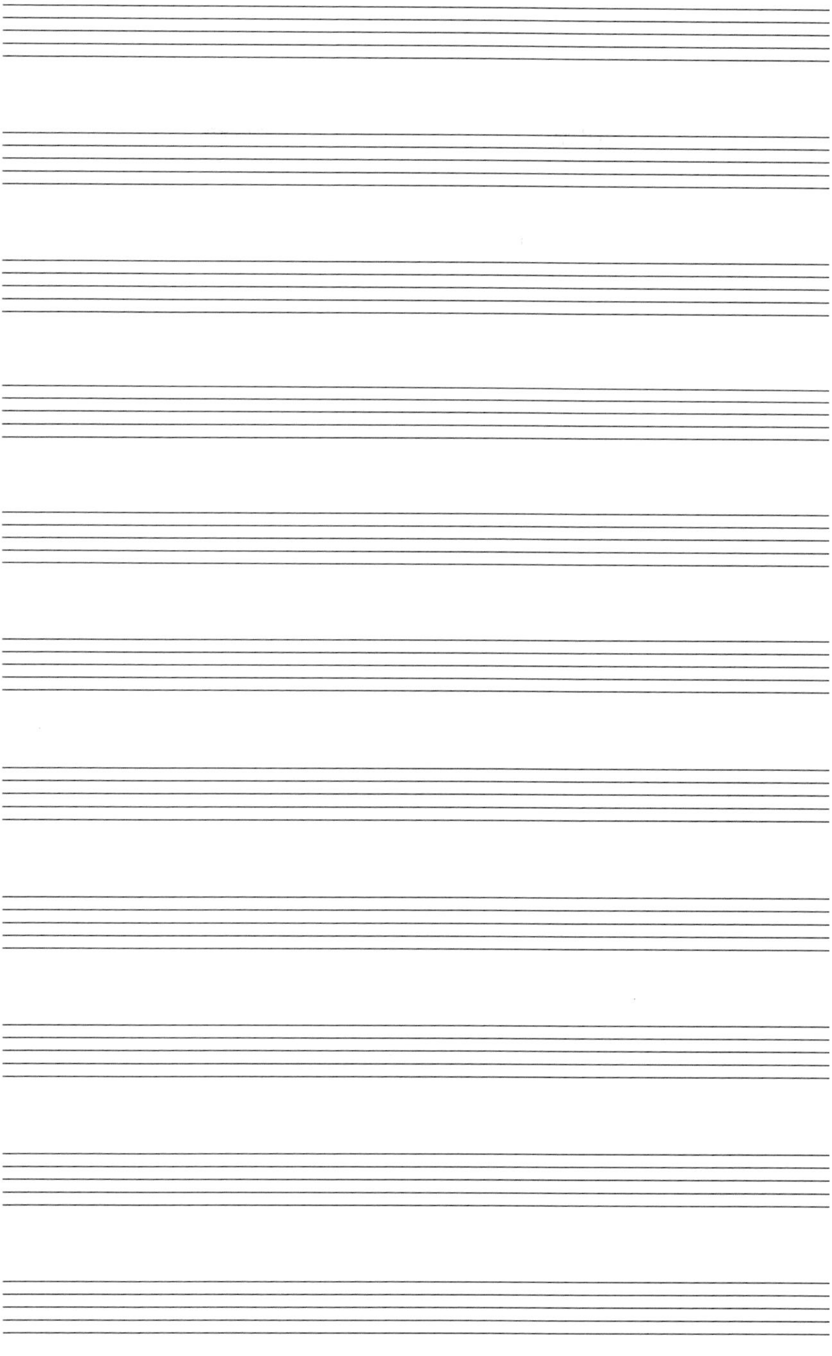

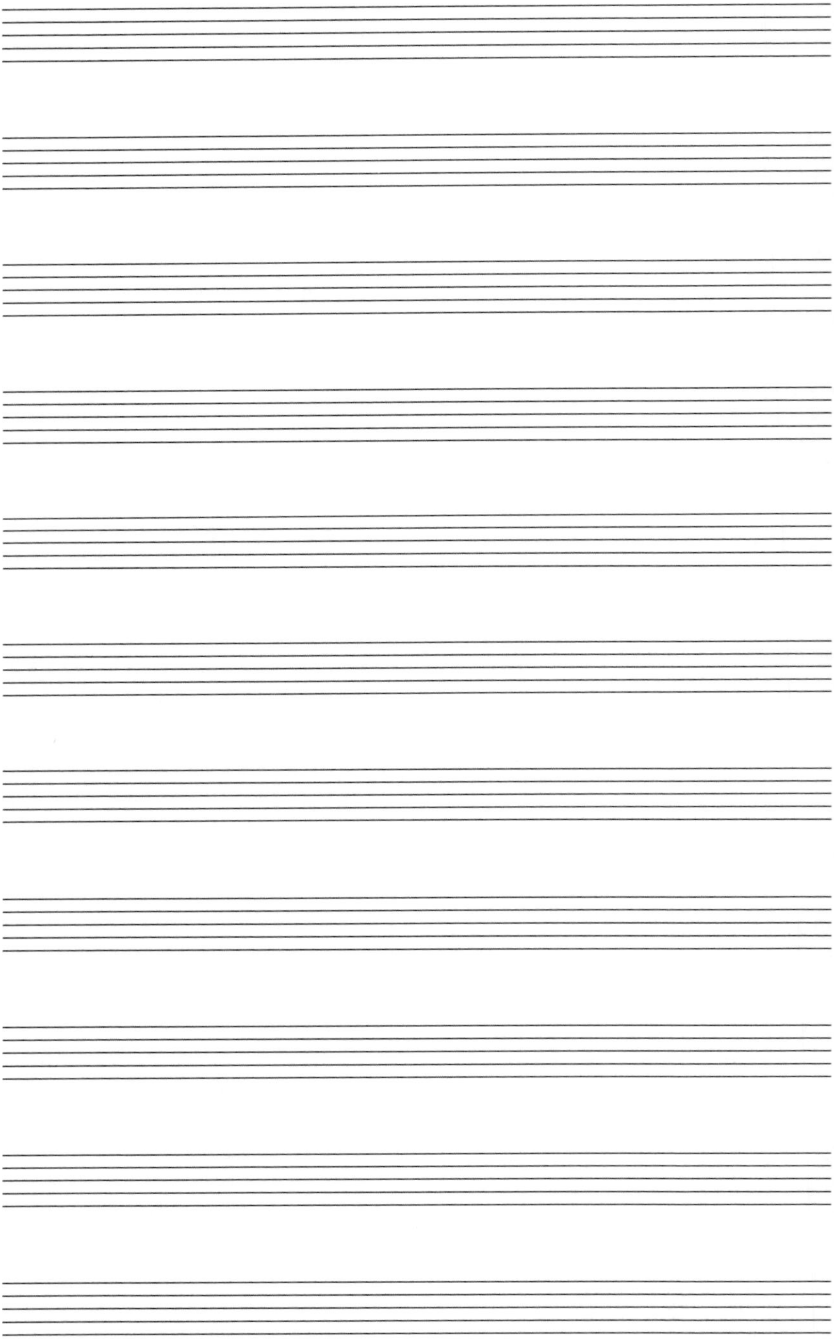

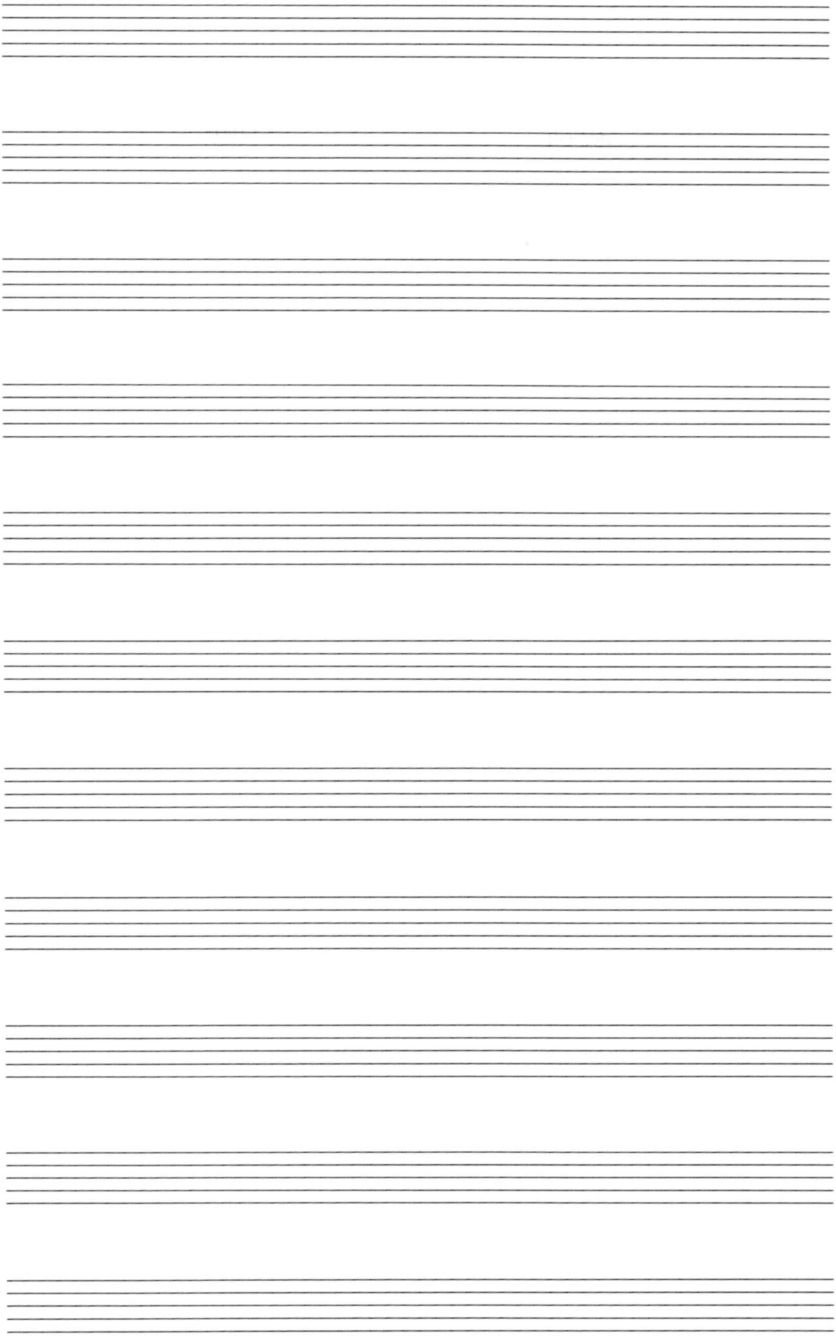

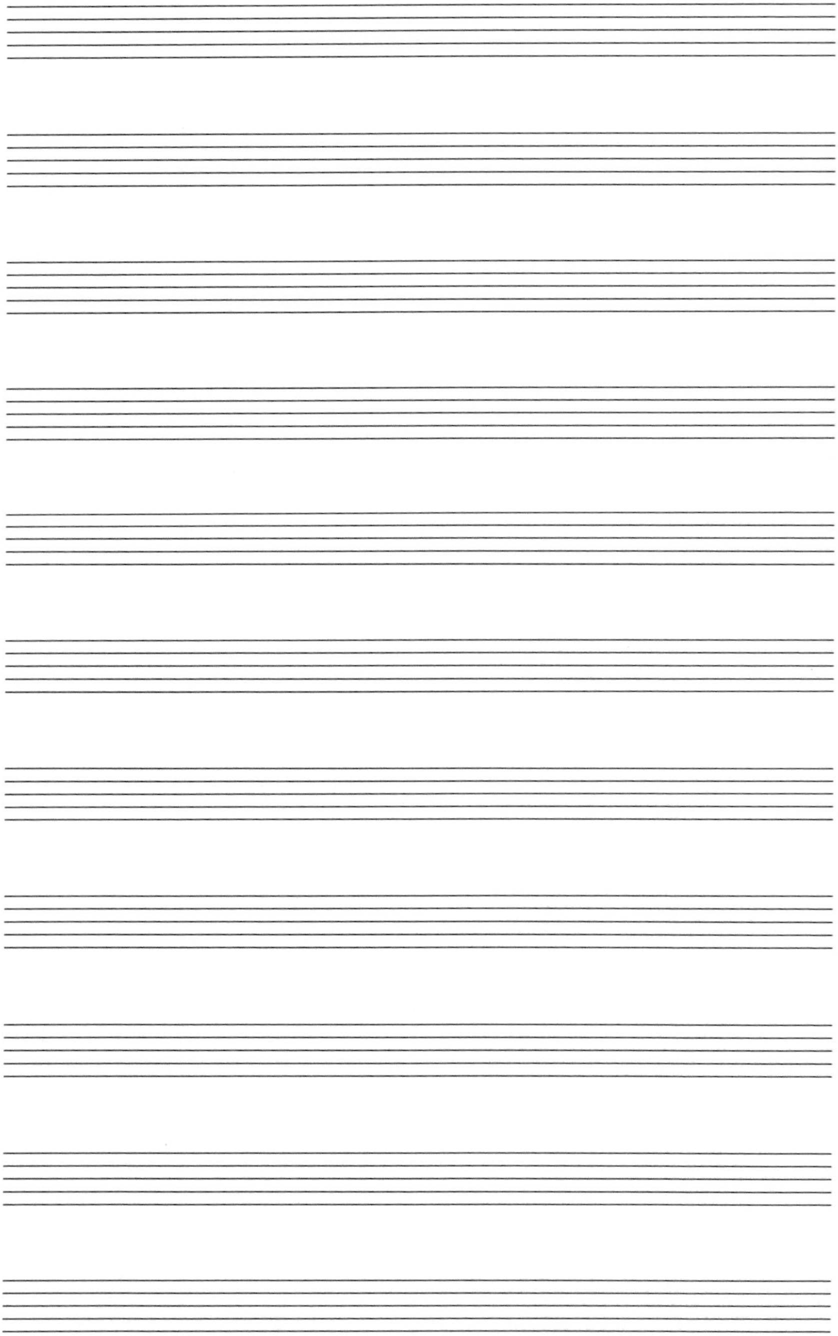

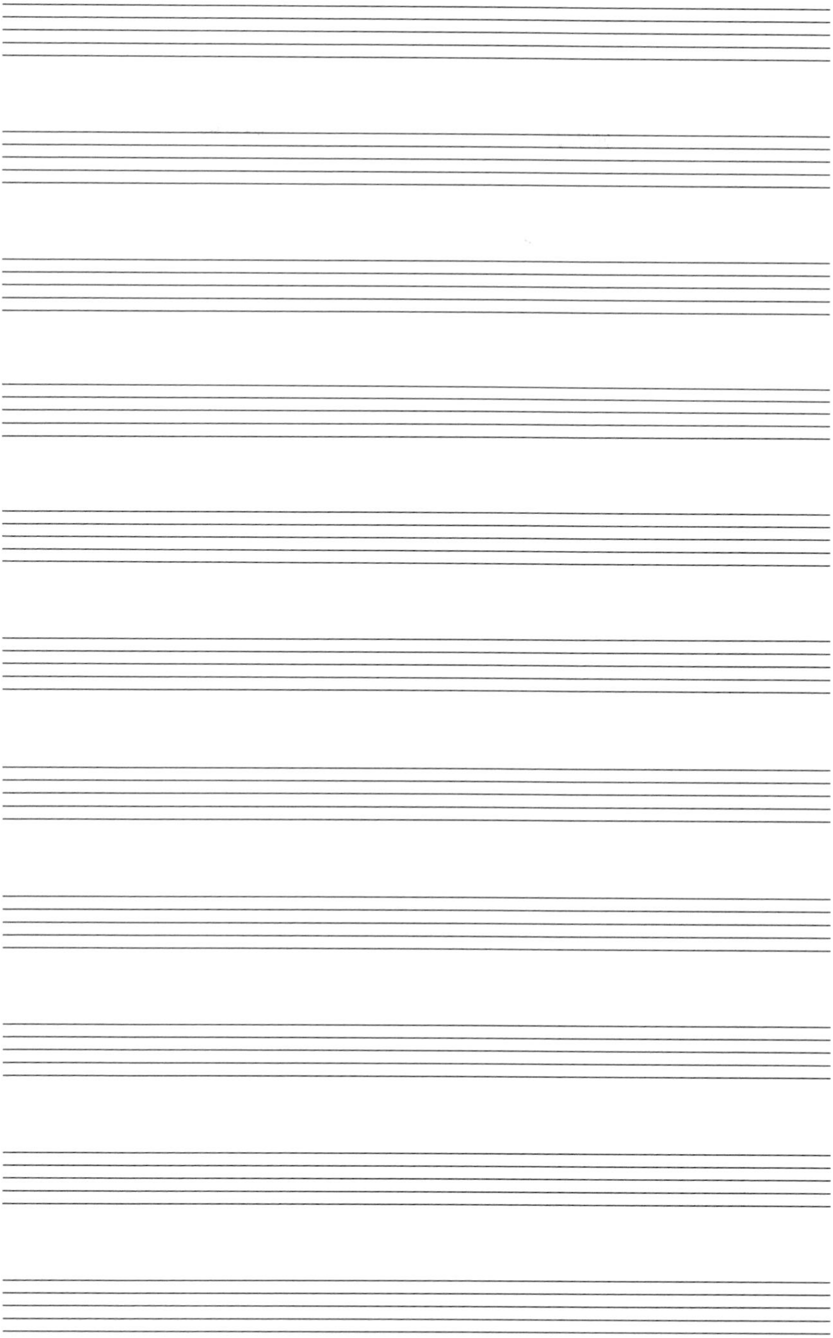

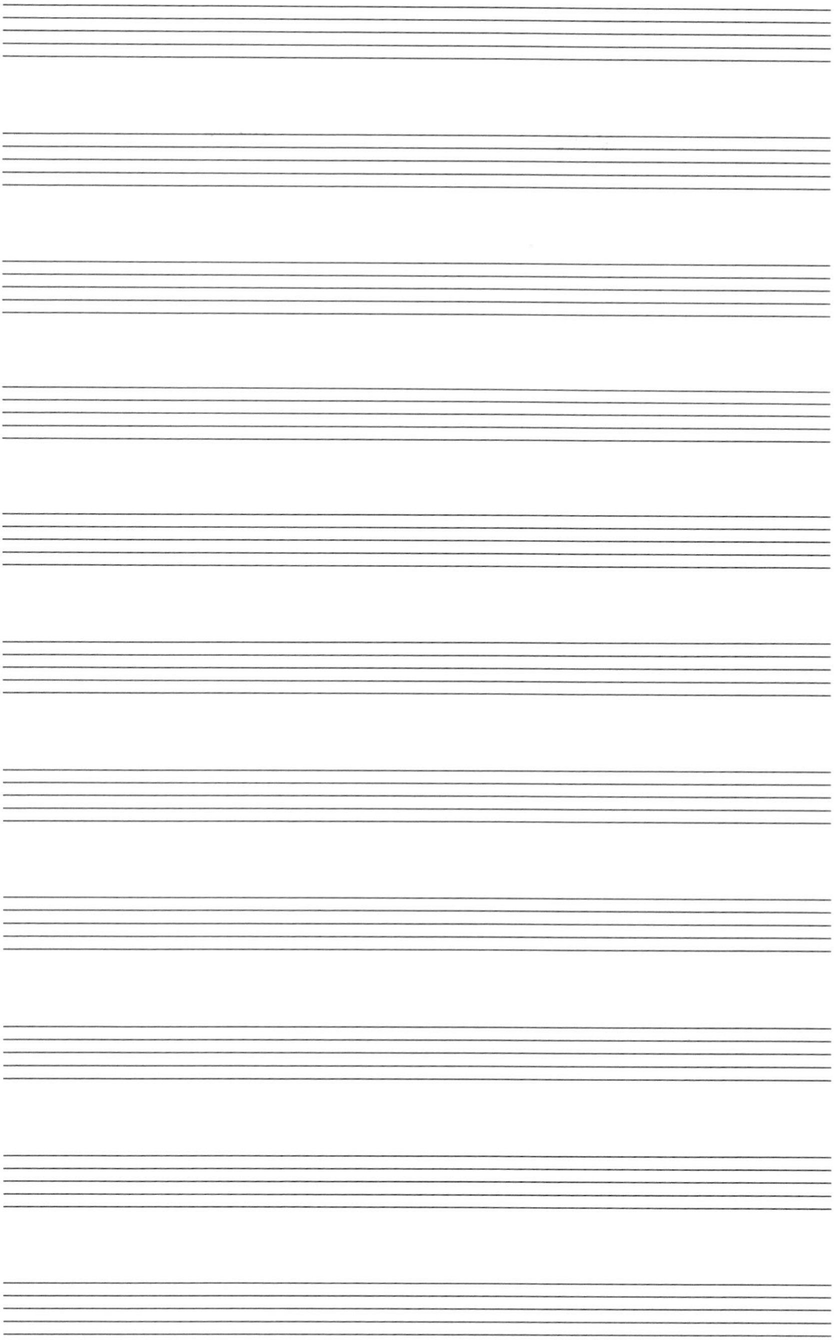

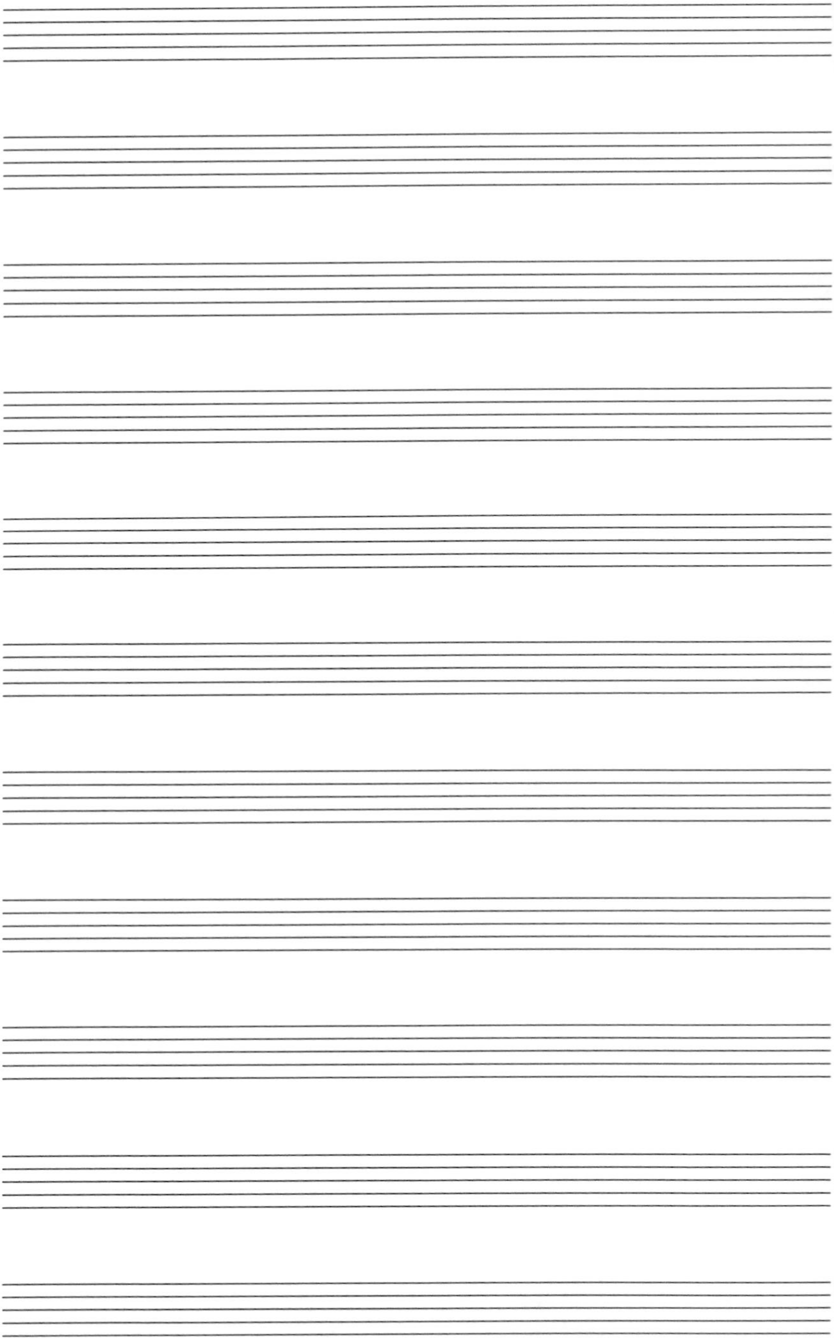

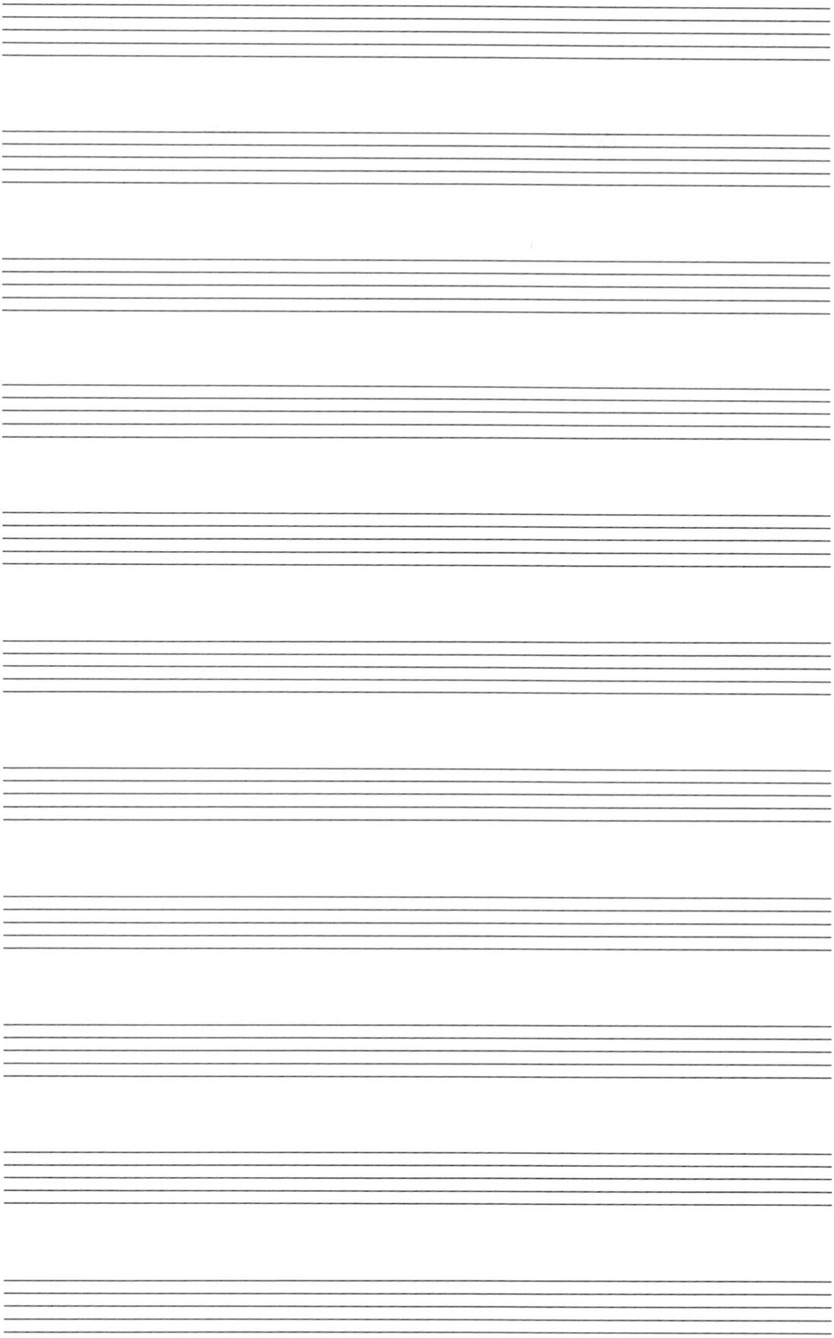

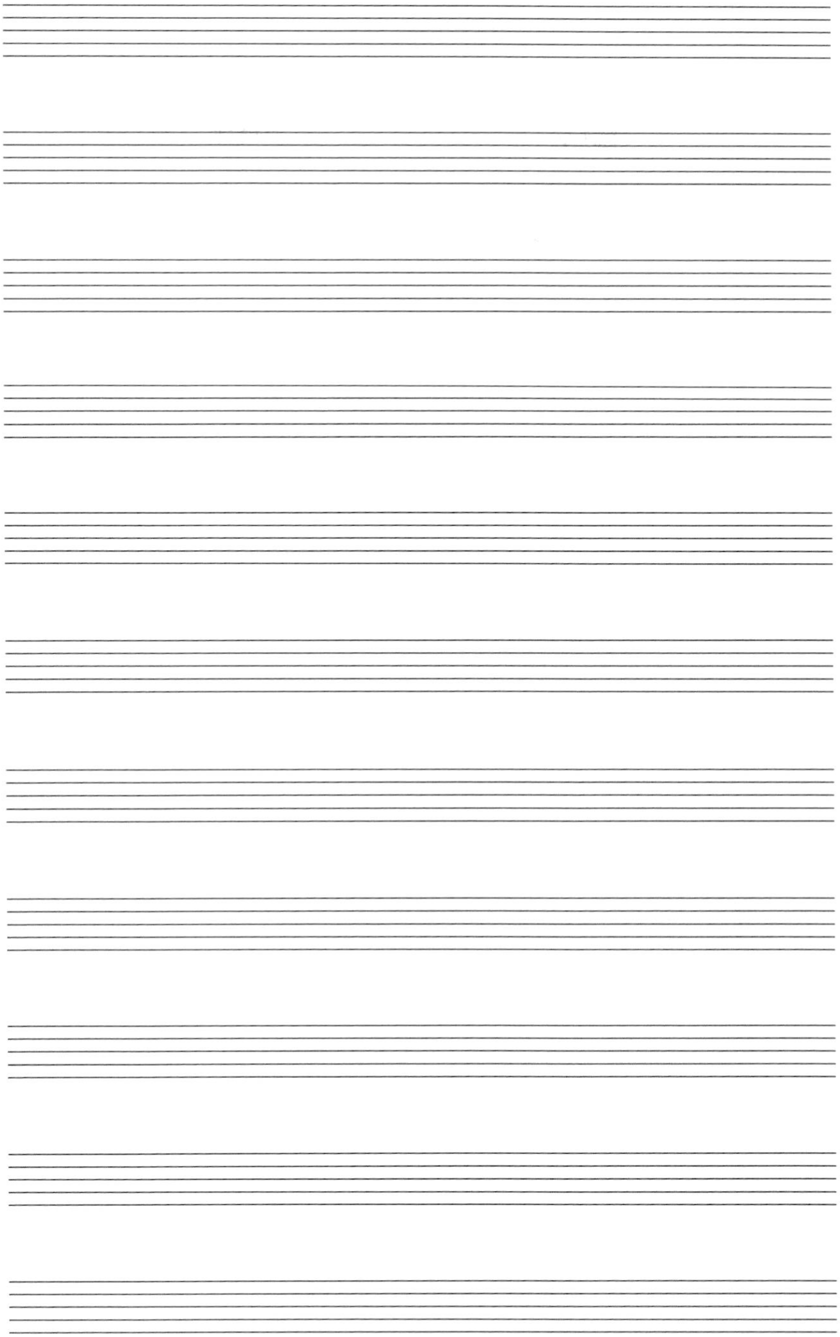

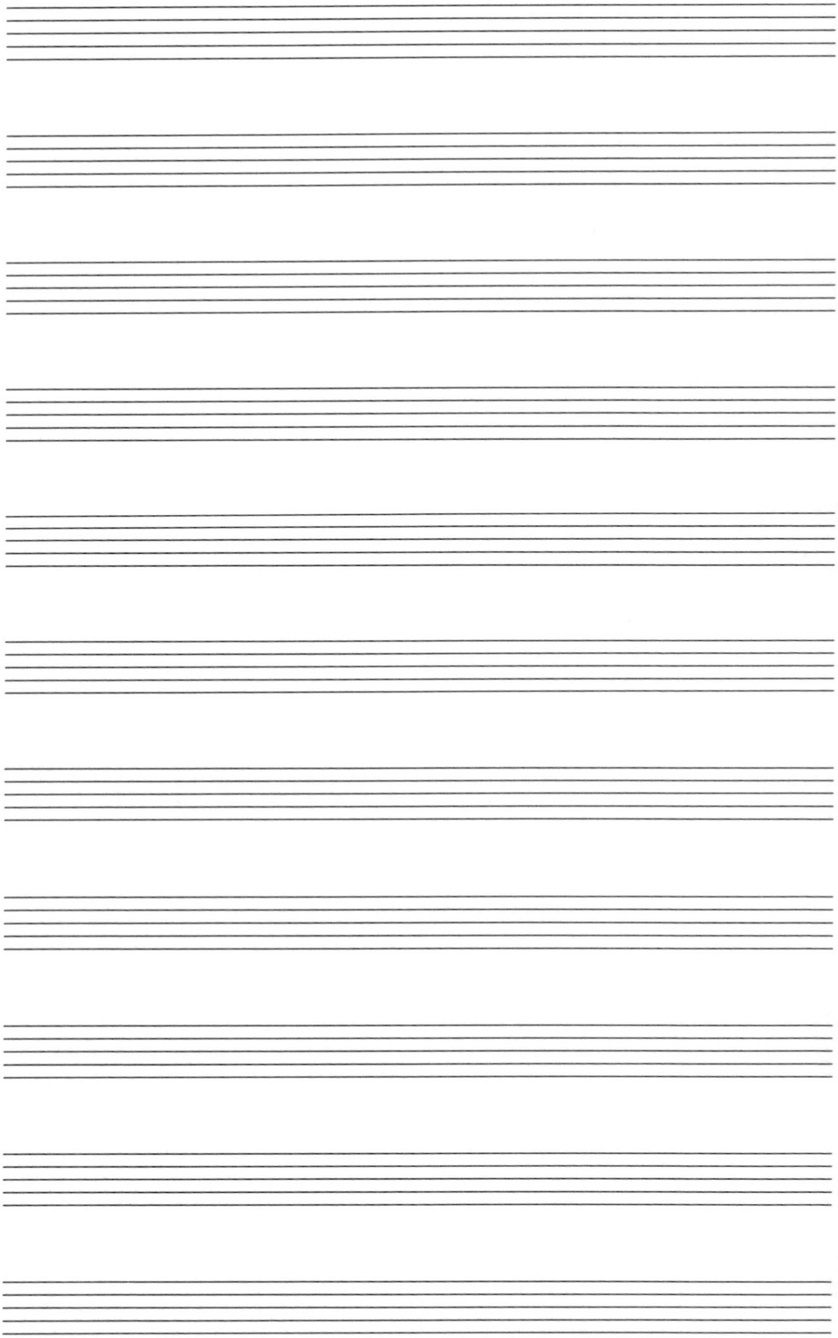

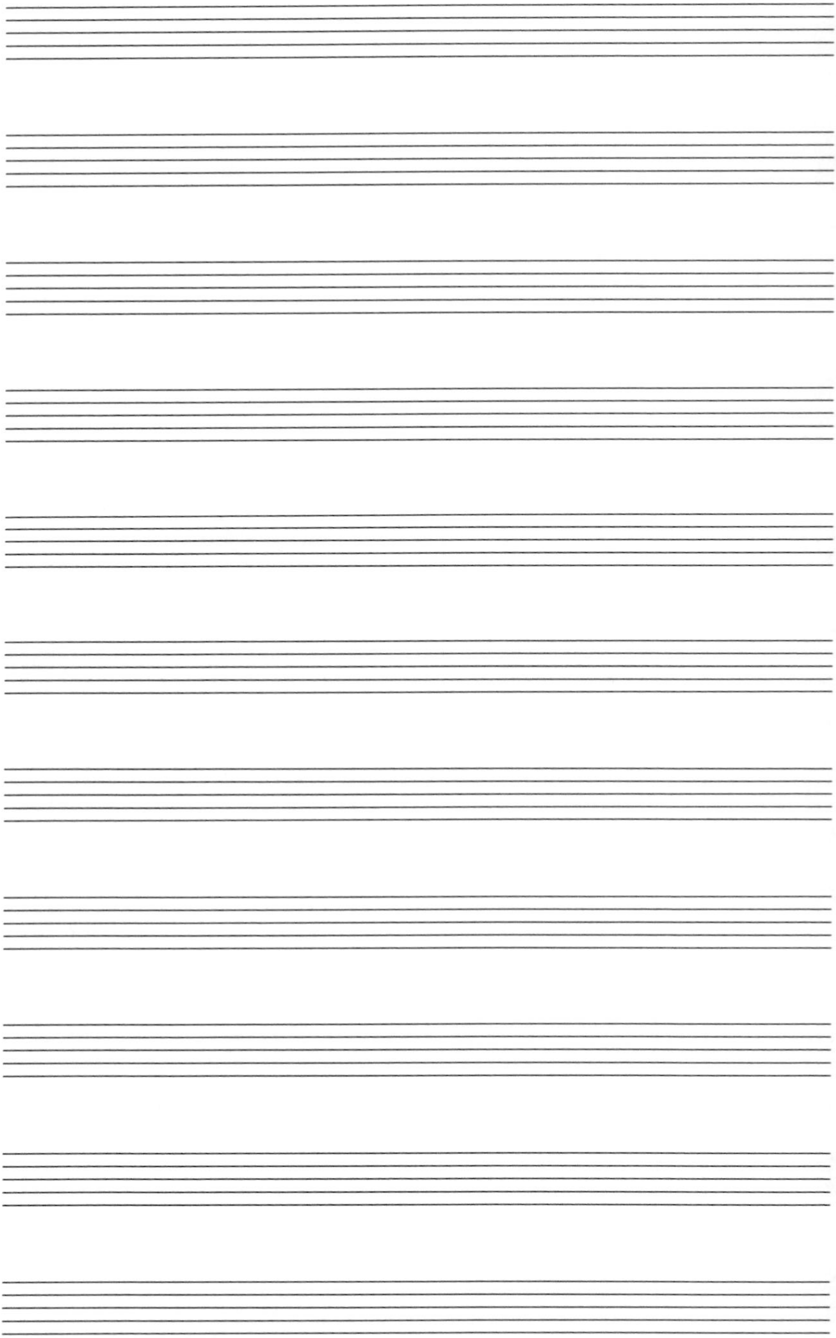

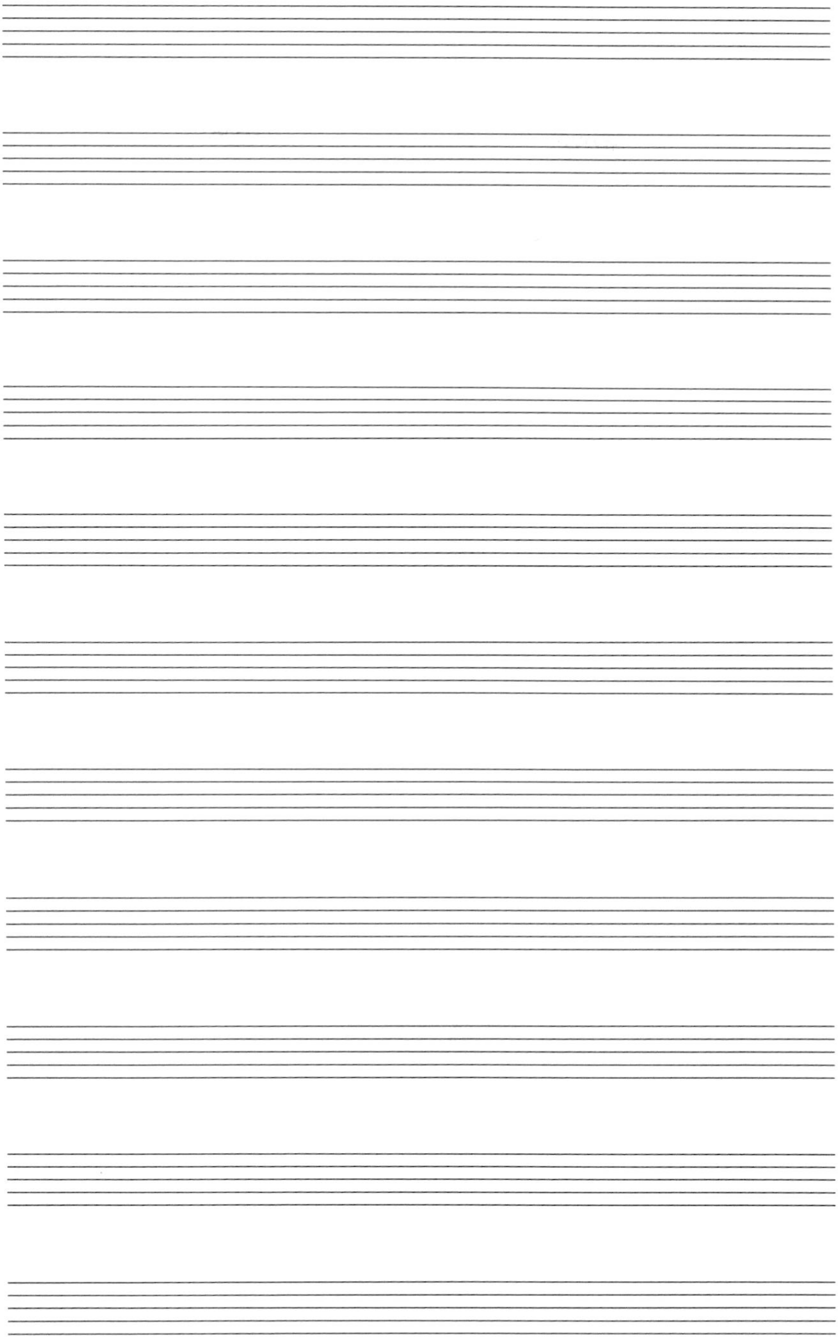

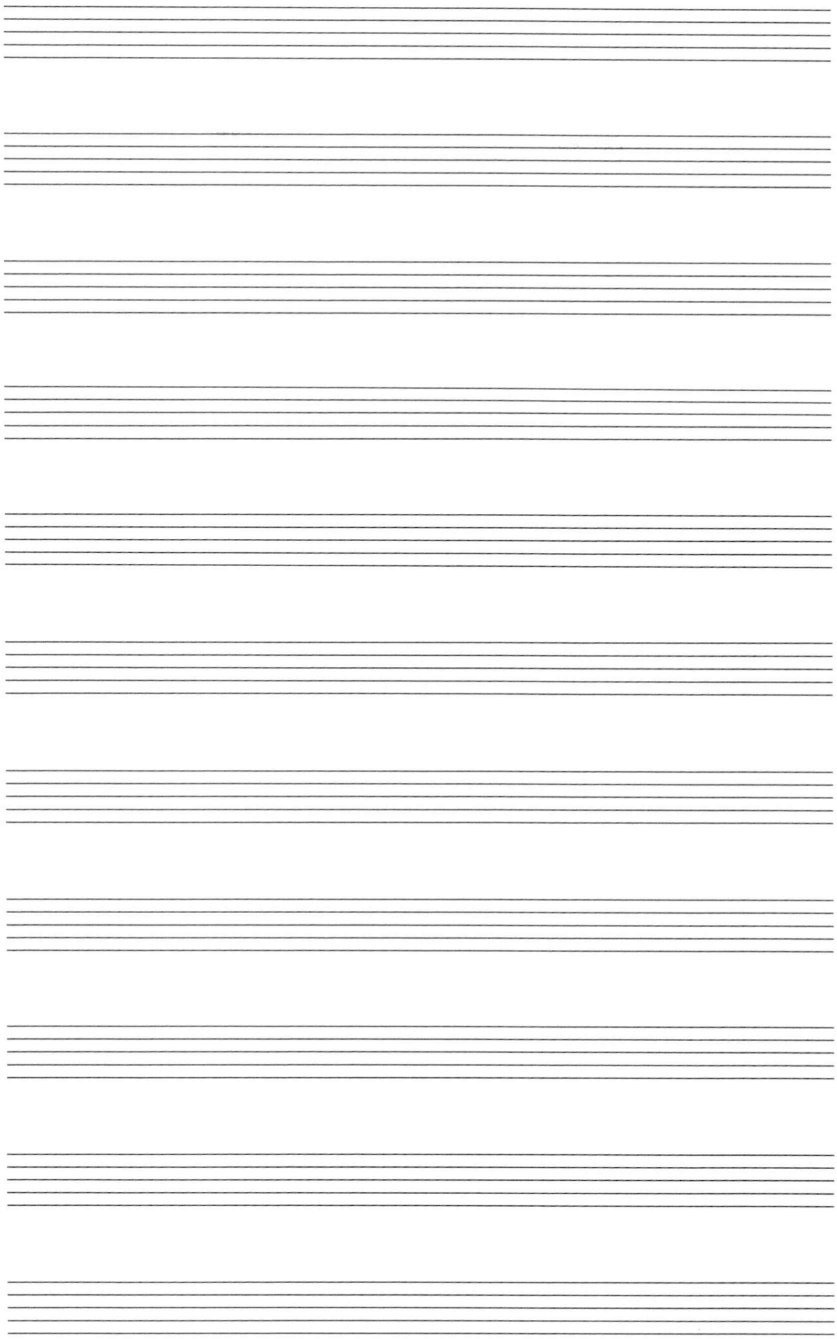

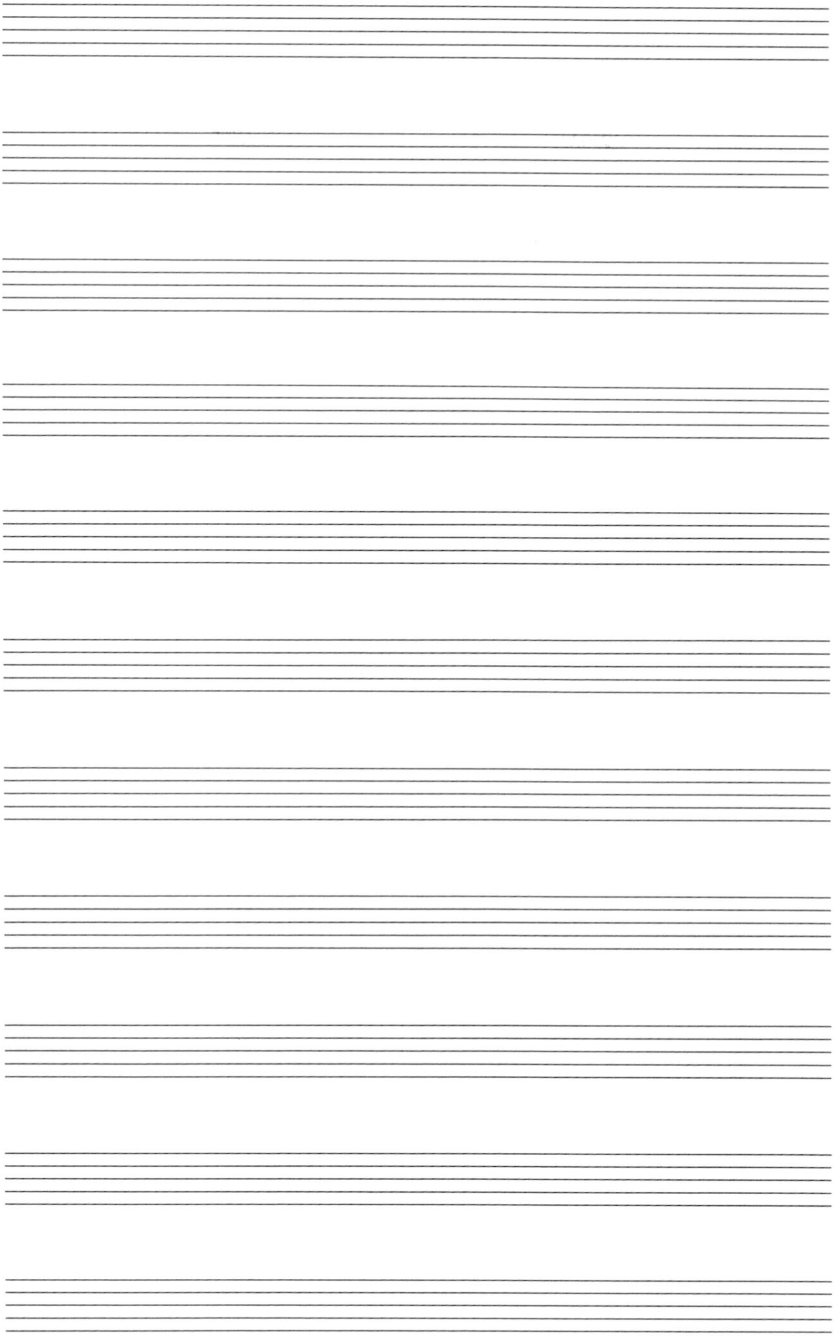

41819416R00057

Made in the USA
Middletown, DE
23 March 2017